GW00546732

Village
Style

English
Countryside
in Camera 2

Village
Style

John Vince

LONDON

IAN ALLAN LTD

To ALAN RANNIE, FSA
– who pointed the way

First published 1974

ISBN 0 7110 0489 7

© John Vince 1974

Published by Ian Allan Ltd, Shepperton, Surrey
and printed in the United Kingdom by
Balding + Mansell Ltd, London and Wisbech

Contents

Preface

Library shelves are lined with books about English villages. This fact will not surprise those already acquainted with the village scene as there is so much for the traveller to see. From the days of King Alfred, English villages changed hardly at all for centuries on end. By Tudor times, however, men began to alter the appearance of the feudal village by enclosing the common fields which formed the basis of village economy. In Georgian England the process was carried further and the landscape took on its present patchwork appearance. Open countryside gave way to a jig-saw of fields with their endless hedgerows and stately elms. Now the hedges are being grubbed up and the elm is under attack from a fungus passed on by bark beetles.

As the landscape changed all those years ago, so did village society. Squires became attracted to the goings-on in London and Bath. Slowly new fashions began to creep into rural England. Local masons and carpenters adapted the 'new fangled' ideas and blended them with their own established traditions. This is the origin and the essence of a village style, which stands quite apart from the nuances of the town dweller's surroundings.

One of the most important visual differences arises from the fact that the appearance of any settlement originally depended upon the type of building materials available close at hand. Later canals and railways made it possible for brick and slate to infiltrate areas previously dominated by stone, timber or clay. Since Georgian times the village has been slowly changing. In the last two decades the pace of change has accelerated. Many villages have been swamped by a tide of 'development' which has robbed them of their village ethos. This visual spoilation is avoidable. History may judge some twentieth-century architects and planners to have been ill versed in the village style that has been evolving for about a millenium.

This book may leave many things unsaid, but to those with eyes to see, it attempts to provide a glimpse of the many faces of the village.

1

The Village Scene

English villages like people possess their own characters. They are all different. Some are unashamed extroverts with very definite inclinations towards flamboyance, others prefer to remain quietly aloof. Certain of their number possess an erect, almost military bearing and it has to be admitted that there are those which are just plain dull. Most, however, have comfortable homely qualities which cloak a wealth of fascination, only revealed when you really get to know them. To uncover the secrets which tell us so much about the village's past you need to use your eyes.

There is an unmistakable and typically English reluctance to dismantle or remove anything which has been in the same place for more than a decade or two. This characteristic has allowed the village to accumulate buildings of all kinds from quite distant times. Along with the architecture, which depended upon the local craftsman's timeless tradition,

a host of miscellaneous fixtures, fittings and decorations has also endured.

The impression the visitor will receive from a first glance at a village street will depend upon the kind of building materials the early villagers had close at hand some thousand years ago. It was in those far off days that so many of the quirks and curves of the village street first appeared. The original dwellings have long since perished but the wayward twisting street may well possess a form which is older than the parish church itself. A street curving uphill probably represents the easiest route a cart could follow. Simple and uncomplicated practical considerations of this kind are easily forgotten in an age when men prefer to travel by car.

Villages may huddle around a green where cottage eaves are close enough for whispered confidences to pass. In some the green gave way long since to a cobbled square where markets are still held. Extravagant elongations too can be found stretched out along a shore or river bank. Bolder still, are other villages which stand unrepentant on hills up against the sky, to defy a millenium of winds and searing rain.

The story of the village may be written in stone, clay, timber, thatch, brick or tile – a very tangle of history for the traveller to untwine.

The Unbaked Earth

There are several corners of England where clay was once used for walls. In Devon the

Atherington, Devon: In the West Country clay walls go by the name of cob. In order to endure, a clay wall must have a good 'hat' and sound 'shoes'. Walls of clay seldom have the strength to support a heavy roof unless they are very thick and for this reason we usually associate cob with thatch. Stability has been added by the buttress. The chimneys provide another point of interest. Two stacks are fashioned in native stone and the third, springing from within the gable, is constructed in brick. Chimney pots began to proliferate in the nineteenth century and the examples seen here are obviously products of mass production. Another feature of importance is the protruding bread oven tucked into the base of the central stack. The use of brick on two of these stacks illustrates the wide variation in colour which this material provides.

name given to this most basic of all building materials is 'cob'. Examples of clay construction can also be found in Hampshire, Wiltshire, the eastern end of Kent, Northamptonshire, Buckinghamshire, Lincolnshire, Yorkshire (out on Holderness), Lancashire, Westmorland and Norfolk. In parts of Norfolk and Suffolk the clay is often made into large bricks – called 'lumps'. These are made, dried and then built into a wall. All clay walls need protection from rainwater and if they are kept dry they will last for ages. One characteristic of clay dwellings is the thickness of their walls. To avoid a point of weakness a clay house may have its corners fashioned into a curve. The techniques of wall construction varied in different areas. Some builders made use of planks (shuttering) and made the wall a layer at a time. This could be a slow process. In Cumberland some 'clay daubins' had their walls raised in a single day. A house formed from unbaked earth often has small irregularities in its walls which a noonday sun in summer will expose as shadows.

ABOVE

Haddenham, Bucks: Sometimes clay is given a particular local name. On the western fringe of Buckinghamshire the white marl is called 'witchert'. This outbuilding shows how timber could be used to provide a gable. The chimney is made from brick – a material more resistant to heat. At the top of the wall a course of undressed stone supports the heavy wooden wall plate. Above the gable a modern weathervane reminds us of the way in which our forefathers travelled.

BELOW

Horwood, Devon: Another cob house with several features of interest. The upper windows which appear at various levels suggest an irregular disposition of the internal floors. At ground level the sash windows are equally divided, but the first-floor windows have shallow upper 'halves' which can be difficult to manipulate. A stone chimney rises from the long wall and its wide interior is protected by two slates which make a typical and effective watershed. The sides of a cob building seldom have a perfectly flat surface and this allows the daylight to cast all kinds of interesting shadows. To help rain water run off the apex of the gable the thatch is swept upwards.

9

Pylle, Somerset: Not all render has an attractive appearance. Uncoloured cement finishes can be flat and visually unexciting. This pair of cottages has an unquestionably modern look with metal-framed windows and brick chimneys. The thatch, however, preserves the link with tradition. This example bears two interesting ornaments which are really a subtle visual joke. Whoever saw a fox walking away from a strutting pheasant?

Haddenham, Bucks: This witchert house provides us with a contrast in styles. Its casement windows, which probably replace older iron and lead counterparts, are neatly finished with lancet heads derived from Gothic fashion. The doorcase, however, is inspired by eighteenth-century ideas with its classical columns supporting the doorhead. Not all iron railings disappeared in World War II and we should be grateful to see that these simple blacksmith-made palings have endured. The gateposts are interesting as their inverted-trident design makes them effective without being overpowering.

Thaxted, Essex: A typical combed-plaster finish arranged in panels. Work of this kind adds considerable visual interest to a street scene. Here we may note the larger window next to the door which probably lights a living room. An alternative to plaster is weatherboarding, which the cottage in the background with its pretty bow illustrates so well. Compare the graceful lines of the bow with the heavy look of the bay protruding from the gable (left). The gas lamp on the corner helps to remind us that in Victorian times a good many larger villages even had their own gas works.

BELOW

Clay walls have to be quite thick in order to support the weight of the roof and the joists which bear the weight of the upper floor. This decaying wall allows us to see how close to the outer surface the joist really was.

BELOW

Nayland, Suffolk: The art of pargetting takes many forms. This example has heraldic inclinations with two chevrons at its base. In the early modern period members of the merchant class who had aspirations to higher things began to become interested in heraldic bearings – a sign of nobility. When they embellished their homes heraldic allusions began to influence the designs they employed. In place of a crest above the shield we see here a cherub which often appears on Jacobean memorial tablets. Two serpents serve as supporters and at the base a rather curious duck's foot emerges.

Stone

Some of the finest English houses are fashioned in stone. At the time of the Norman Conquest stone was used only for buildings of importance like the parish church or the manor house. The wealth of the wool merchants in the Middle Ages helped stone to move down the social scale. Any traveller across the Cotswolds will know what fine buildings they bequeathed to us. England's best building stone is found in the long belt of Jurassic limestone which stretches from Lyme Bay to the Humber. This soft stone allowed the masons to fashion the splendid details which we associate with the buildings along its course.

Sandstone too is a soft material. It has one disadvantage when used externally; the elements wear it away at a rapid rate. There are several kinds of sandstone and part of its architectural interest derives from the varying colours to be found. In the west it is pink or red; Bedfordshire provides yellowish-brown.

Deep rusty browns can be found in Northamptonshire, and Yorkshire provides browns of a lighter shade. Other kinds can be found in Norfolk where the local name used is 'carstone'. Great houses – like Wallington, Northumberland – were constructed in sandstone, but it has also been employed as a roofing material on quite humble dwellings in Derbyshire, Sussex and Herefordshire.

The millstone grits of the Pennines and the granite of Devon and Cornwall presented a harder face to the mason's chisel. Buildings fashioned in these stones have the plainest look of all.

Marsh Gibbon, Bucks: A house in the Cornbrash area of Buckinghamshire. Cornbrash was quarried in thin slabs. Walls made from it have a rough texture. The term rubblestone is used to describe them. This house has old-style wooden lintels. Most of its windows are nineteenth-century casements, but where the solitary sash is to be seen we can guess there was once a door. Long ago this was probably two dwellings.

ABOVE

*Haddenham, Bucks: More obvious signs of change can be seen
on this house where the brick dressings of two former doorways
are still quite prominent. The doorway and the two small
windows flanking it are clearly late additions to the original
structure. Below the eaves on the right we can see what is
probably the oldest window with three leaded lights and
diamond panes. In contrast the other windows on the ground
floor have a blank 'unseeing' look which comes from their large
single panes. An assortment of small panes adds texture to a
window which a single sheet of glass can never possess. The
unusual quality of the wooden tracery in the small windows and
the detail of the porch derives from the fact that this was once
the home of Walter Rose – author of* The Village Carpenter
and Good Neighbours.

BELOW

*West Country: This cottage has a definite ecclesiastical air.
The gable seems to belong to the fourteenth century with its ogee
head and supporting pinnacles (the one on the right has fallen).
Following the dissolution of the monasteries in Henry VIII's
reign a good many deserted religious houses became quarries for
the local populace. This example, however, may have been
built on to what remained of a remote chapel.*

Chapmanslade, Wilts: A curious house with three storeys – an unusual feature in a village. Brick corners (quoins) support rubblestone walls. There is some evidence of alterations to the front where window openings have been blocked at first- and second-floor levels. Below the lipped gable there is a row of old bottles built into the wall as decoration. Their bases appear as dots which resemble the following Roman numerals MVIII (to the left of the window) and XXI. What this cryptic inscription means is not immediately obvious. Perhaps it is intended to be the date 1821. This is correctly rendered in Roman notation as MDCCCXXI. If the builder intended the VIII to represent the odd hundreds, however, he was able to dispense with the awkward curves of DCCC and save himself room and extra bottles.

Sutton-under-Brailes, Warwicks: In common with so many stone houses this one has brick chimneys which rise from a thatch as smooth as velvet. The circular bread oven reminds us of the days when cottagers were almost self-sufficient and always baked their own bread.

ABOVE

Eaton, Leics: Softer stone can be more easily worked into regular blocks and it then becomes possible to construct even courses which give a house a distinctly different appearance. The sash windows are carefully spaced in the classical manner and care has been taken to see that the central window matches the width of the doorway – hence it is three panes wide. All window and door openings are set in ashlared dressings. The window ledges are set at a steep angle to make sure that rainwater is quickly expelled. A six-panelled door helps us to place the date of building in the earlier part of the nineteenth century.

BELOW

Horbling, Lincs: Limestone and pantiles always make an agreeable combination. The sash windows are not as old as the stonework and it is interesting to note the differences between those in the upper and lower floors. A sundial – see page 35 – adds a final flourish to the simple lines of the composition. Such things were a symbol of status in the eighteenth century.

ABOVE

Erlestoke, Wilts: Limestone comes in various colours and once it has been incorporated into a wall the elements take over and gradually its appearance begins to change. Rainwater slowly washes away some of the chemicals which determine a stone's colour. This is why the stones on the lower part of the wall have a lighter look. Where the deep eaves protect the wall, less of the original colour has been washed away. In common with the house at Horbling (page 15) the ground-floor windows have heavy stone lintels. The leaded windows sit comfortably in their iron frames. On the upper floor handsome round-headed windows, which speak of the Georgian era, are protected by well-proportioned gables complete with deeply scalloped barge boards. Above the door with its deeply carved hood we can see another unusual feature – a false window. On the left even the modern garage echoes this feature in a most tasteful manner.

BELOW

Uffington, Berks: From the lower levels of the chalklands the hardest variety of chalkstone is obtained. This stone was used for hundreds of buildings on the chalklands. You cannot mistake the whiteness of chalkstone when it is used. The corners of a chalk wall are often strengthened by brick quoins as this example shows. Brick is also employed for the chimneys. At the rear the roof sweeps down to cover a single-storey addition to the ground floor. Notice how the thatcher has formed a half-hipped area at the top of the gable. This cast some rainwater to the side and therefore caused less to be discharged at the corners – an important consideration where soft stone was used. Such a feature not only contributes to a building's preservation but enhances its appearance.

Flint

As long ago as the Stone Age, men were busy in these islands fashioning flints into weapons and tools. Such was the demand for this material that men burrowed underground to secure a supply. Those who wish to explore that subject further should visit Grimes Graves, Norfolk – a site now in the care of the Ministry of Works. Although flint can be fractured into razor-like slivers its very hardness made it the most durable of building materials. Flints, however, present certain problems to the builder as two are never alike. The reason for this derives from the fact that flint was formed by an amalgamation of chemicals (silica) in the cracks underground.

Castle builders – at Pevensey and Portchester – made use of flint as long ago as the third century AD. A millenium or so later flint was in vogue once more by church builders. Flint occurs in many parts of England. It can be found from Wiltshire across to Kent, and in Berkshire and Surrey. Northwards from the Thames it spills across East Anglia. Its northern and western boundary runs along the line made by the Chiltern scarp.

When flint is examined, a hard crust of chalk can be seen on its outer surface. Neolithic man was interested in the black core and knew how to reduce each stone to a required number of flakes. Builders too saw the possibilities of making use of the inner blackness. A broken stone could provide an interesting contrast to the whiteness of the flint's natural surface. The use of 'knapped' flint in the medieval period provided us with magnificent structures like the Gatehouse at St Osyth's, Essex. Flint was often combined with stonework and from the eighteenth century onwards with brick. Sometimes stone and brick is limited to quoins and window or door openings. The most effective combination of stone and flint will be found where the chequered arrangement is favoured.

It is not surprising to find that place names are sometimes derived from the presence of flint deposits. There is a Flintham in Nottinghamshire and a Flinton in the East Riding of Yorkshire. Both, however, lie outside the areas renowned for flint building.

Chilterns: A Victorian estate cottage in brick, flint and tile. The extravagance of the chimney stack is in marked contrast to the paucity of the glazing in the windows. To the left we can just see the chimney of the wash-house which contained the copper used for the weekly wash. Electricity is a modern necessity and here the supply comes via the inelegant pole just outside the garden fence. When Victorian designers planned cottages like this they seem to have been more concerned with external appearance than the housewife's needs.

Timber

Almost every county except Cornwall and those in the extreme north can provide us with examples of timber-framed houses. Timber was the material used by the peasant in the days when the manorial lord enjoyed stone. Eventually the techniques of timber building improved and there came a time when English carpenters could fashion the most magnificent structures.

Early timber houses had panels filled with a wattle framework which lent support to the clay 'daub'. Timber houses no doubt originally had thatched roofs. These days tiles will frequently be found instead. A timber house had its framework made in the carpenter's yard where the various parts were numbered so that they could easily be identified on the building site. The framing marks used by the carpenter were sometimes simply Roman numerals. Ancient structures can be found where symbols serve instead. Where they occur their shapes seem to suggest the ancient Runic letters which go back to the Saxon period. We know that masons used their own secret symbols which can still be seen on church stonework. It is not very difficult to imagine that perhaps the master carpenters of old 'borrowed' such signs for their own use.

LEFT

Thaxted, Essex: Brick, flint, tiles and sandstone pebbles form the basis of this rather shaky looking dwelling of the one up and down variety. The single row of bricks at each corner does little to inspire confidence in stability and the leaning roof adds to the feeling of insecurity. Although a sash is still to be seen upstairs its fellow seems to have been replaced with a cheaper casement. Dark brown pebbles are used at each side of the simple plank door and the more elaborate lozenge next to the window no doubt looked more convincing when the structure was in better repair. Evidence of disuse grows upon the doorstep.

BELOW

A hall house from Boughbeech in Kent during its reconstruction at the Singleton Open Air Museum, Sussex. Two of the panels have been plastered, but the remainder show the wattle frame. Its unglazed windows are divided by bars. To some eyes these Wealden houses are the most splendid of all our timbered buildings.

*Nayland, Suffolk: Among the different styles of timber build-
ings those with a 'jetty' (a protruding upper storey) are probably
the most attractive. East Anglia is particularly rich in houses of
this kind and this row shows us several interesting characteristics. The frames of the upper floor are strengthened by heavy
curved diagonal braces at the corners. In this style of framing
the position of the window was more or less a fixed factor. At
ground level one house retains a visible timber frame. The
neighbour (on the right) has had its framework replaced by
brick. On the other side, however, the 'timbers' are false, but
they do add continuity to the total impression. Casement
windows are common on timber houses but the house on the
extreme right has a sliding casement on its ground floor and
upon the gable.*

*Erlestoke, Wilts: Houses with this kind of structure are
usually described as box-framed. In contrast to the Suffolk style
the braces are smaller and straight. Again they occur in the
upper storey. The panels are now filled with bricks, arranged in
herring-bone fashion, which replaced the original wattle and
daub infill. A vast thatch, looking like a Norman helmet with a
protruding nasal, completes the design. Notice how the gable is
half-hipped which allows the corner of the roof to curl round
and carry rainwater well clear of the vulnerable corner. The
intention of the deep pendant nasel of thatch was to carry water
clear of the front door. Since the erection of the tiled porch its
function has been superceded. Once again a utilitarian pole
detracts from the photographer's intended composition.*

Aldbury, Herts: Brick infill can vary in quality and the poorest examples occur when the bricks are as large as our present standard version. Those used here, however, are thin and therefore old. A diamond-paned leaded casement graces this gable but below the jetty there is a later version in wood.

South Midlands: It is difficult to appreciate just how a roof stays up until you actually take a close look at its structure. Buildings are re-roofed at very infrequent intervals and this photograph was taken, sad to say, during the demolition of an eighteenth-century barn which made way for a concrete replacement. There are various methods of keeping a roof in place and the one shown here is simple but very effective. On the wooden framework of the walls rests the heavy tie-beam (t). Braces (b) spring from the tie-beam to a point where the purlin (p) and principal rafter (r) coincide. To add strength to the structure windbraces (w) are mortised into the principal rafter and the purlin. The battens above the rafters provided fixings for the tiles.

South Midlands: There is an old saying about half a loaf being better than none. From this strange mixture of styles we could get the impression that a former owner started to rebuild his timber-framed house and ran out of money half-way. The sash windows, slate roof and round-headed door suggest the early part of the nineteenth century, but the timbered half is obviously a good deal older. Notice how the window above the doorway is three panes wide – just like the example noted at Eaton, Leics (page 15). From this unusual house we can see how much the pitch of a slate roof differed from that of tiles – which usually followed the slope of an even earlier thatch.

BOTTOM RIGHT

Erlestoke, Wilts: One of the interesting variations to be found in many old village settings is the manner in which our forefathers arranged their separate dwellings. Today's 'planners' seem to think only in straight lines. Where a gable faces a roadway, however, the usual line of ridges is broken and this adds a good deal to the visual qualities of the scene. A gable enriched with barge boards, mural tablets (just below the window), an unusual casement and a rich but simple base of topiary can only add to our pleasure. In common with its neighbours the brickwork has been coloured white. Thatch too is a pleasing texture which complements the usual tile. Very often brick is simply a covering for an older structure. The gable on the left reveals the building's original framework, and we can readily appreciate the depth of the brick skin which faces the road. It is the variation in the size of different buildings and the variety of the materials from which they are formed which provides us with the very essence of the village's visual character.

ABOVE

Corrugated iron is about the worst thing that can happen to a building visually speaking. In the 1920s a great number of cottages were re-roofed in this medium for reasons of simple economy. The timber frame of this dwelling is supported on a base of limestone which was also used for the chimney.

Brick

We have to thank the Romans for introducing brick to our shores. The technique of firing bricks seems to be almost five thousand years old. There are still fragments of Roman brick to be found in England. Every year the plough exposes some to the sunlight. A few buildings still contain Roman brick – like the Saxon church at Brixworth, Northants. The village name has nothing to do with bricks incidentally. When the Romans departed their buildings slowly decayed and were eventually forgotten.

Bricks seem to have been re-introduced into England late in the thirteenth century. They may have come from the Low Countries as ballast in ships returning home to East Anglia. There is also some evidence to support the idea that they were again being made in England at that time, see Alec Clifton-Taylor, op. cit. We can be more sure of the use made of brickwork, two hundred years later, as a variety of buildings from that period still survive, eg Ewelme School, Oxon (*not shown*). To begin with brick was used by gentlemen of fashion. Very slowly, like other materials mentioned above, brick moved down the social scale until in the eighteenth and nineteenth centuries it was commonly used for the labouring man's cottage. Brick encompasses both the magnificent and the mundane.

The standard brick of today took a long time to evolve. In Tudor England bricks tended to be long and thin. A tax on bricks was imposed in 1784 and it remained until 1850. Nearly a decade later mechanical methods were introduced into the brick-making process. The rate of production then increased and when the Hoffman Kiln (1858) was added to the brickmaker's equipment older hand methods began to become obsolete. Small country brickworks lingered on for a considerable time, however, and some endured until 1939. Then the open-topped kilns were closed down never to work again. Brickfields were often located close to railways or canals which helped the distribution of brick throughout the land. When this stage was reached even traditional materials in shires remote from the brickfields had their ancient supremacy challenged. Economics began to outweigh tradition and a rising tide of convenience washed a permanent pinkness into pastoral England.

Wendover, Bucks: The fact that bricks vary in colour provides us with many important clues. All the buildings shown here are timber-framed, but this truth is almost hidden behind the brick-work. Behind the high carriage doors (left), however, the secret is revealed. The house at the centre has casement windows in contrast to its fellows which possess grander sashes. Both the carriage doors have a loft above – this was often the coachman's sleeping quarters. The window above the right-hand door has been blocked, but its shape cannot escape the camera's eye. Another difference to be noted here is the contrast in the slope and height of the roofs. When a false front was added to an old house and sash windows were introduced the owner had to face a few technical problems. It was impossible to fit two rows of tall sash windows below the old eaves of a thatched house. The only answer was to make the façade con-siderably taller. This had an effect on the pitch of the roof which can be seen here.

BELOW

Aldbury, Herts: Tiles too have a tale to tell. Their colour variations are also a useful guide to alterations or a re-roofing. A change in the colour of the bricks and of the tiles takes a very long time to disappear. From the clues we can glean from this group of cottages it is easy to guess that the twin gables on the right represent an addition.

ABOVE

Midlands: The dull uniformity of the terrace began to creep into the countryside at the time of the Industrial Revolution. Homes had to be found for the workers and those constructed for them were usually very rudimentary. Those shown here have two rooms up and two down.

BELOW

Okeford Fitzpaine, Dorset: One of the fascinating things about English vernacular building is the way in which an assortment of materials is frequently married together. This splendid house with its softly textured thatch has an interesting history. Here mixed in a most delightful way we can see rubblestone, ashlar,

half-timbering, brick and brick nogging – a real symphony of styles. The oldest part is probably the portion to the right – with its chequered stonework – which supports the later timber frame. Facing the roadway the gable provides us with a distinctive texture derived from its alternating courses of large and small stones. The lean-to, composed of brick and stone, provided the thatcher with a problem as its roof has a different pitch. Notice how the thatch protrudes above the doorway to carry the water clear of the wall. All the windows follow the traditional shape of typical casements. A sash window in a design of this kind would introduce a disturbing vertical element which could only clash with the subtle undulation of the ridge. The central chimney is protected by a flat slate raised on four legs in the fashion often found in the West Country and in the North West.

25

ABOVE LEFT
Somersby, Lincs: A brick façade which probably hides an older interior. Three sash windows on the first floor do not coincide with those at ground level in the usual manner. The lower wings are clothed in brickwork, but the shape of their windows hints at the real structure within. Typical pantiles cover all and the variety of chimney pots are obviously of differing ages. Next to the front door modern plumbing introduces a note of discord and declares the function of the room above the doorway. It is curious but true to note that even with the rigours of our English climate indigenous plumbers seem to have a penchant for installing fittings of this kind on the north side of a building.

LEFT
Turweston, Bucks: A limestone house refaced in brick which is tied in at the corners with brick quoins. In our country brick-fields the temperature of the kiln during firing could not be controlled with precision. Variations in temperature produced bricks of different colours. The darker ones used here to make a typical pattern were those 'overdone' during firing. Once again the plumber was unable to hide his essential pipework.

ABOVE
South Downs: Kilns also provided tiles which can protect walls as well as the roof timbers.

2
Streets

Doors

The door is a part of our inheritance which is usually taken for granted. A door, however, has several important functions to perform. It bars the way to strangers who must knock to gain admission; keeps out the worst effects of the weather; and provides an easy means of entrance or exit for the occupants. The ancestor to the door was probably the rough hide hung over the opening and this no doubt derived from the boulder which was once rolled across the entrance of the prehistoric cave.

Village doors today have quite a lot to tell us. Some may be as old as the eighteenth century. Others were made at the end of the Georgian period which was followed by the fashions of the Regency era. There is little difference between the two as far as village doors are concerned. Both styles made use of a door constructed with six panels set in a stout oak frame. This was the pattern which the countryside inherited from the fashionable cities like Bath and London. It came to the village street via the great house set in the squire's park. Along the village street we can find the houses – which were frequently business premises too – of the middle-class residents. These included the merchants, with interest centred on the rural community, and the lesser gentry. Both were concerned with following the fashions set by the 'higher' strata of society. When their timber-framed

houses were given a face lift with brickwork the village carpenter was called in to provide the latest style in windows (sash) and doors. It would be a mistake, of course, to imagine that all the doors of even a middle-class house followed the six-panelled pattern of the front door. Panelled doors in moulded doorcases were to be seen at the entrance to the principal rooms but below stairs or in the attics – where the servants were quartered – elegance gave way to the utility of plainer planks. Fashion dictated that the front door should give the best possible impression but the same ideas were seldom observed at the back which was hidden from public gaze.

Cottagers, of course, did not aspire to anything more than a simple plank door with braces. Such a door served at both front and back. This does not mean that you will never find a six-panelled door attached to a cottage. Over the years grand doors have been 'borrowed' when larger houses were altered or demolished. It is usually easy to decide when a door comes into the latter migrant class. Speculative builders have 'converted' many a Victorian row of cottages into dwellings which estate agents prefer to label 'Georgian'.

The importation of huge quantities of deal from Scandinavia (in the late nineteenth

Two heavily carved brackets support this doorhead and a covering of lead protects it. An imposing arrangement made it essential for the door to follow the six-panel pattern which was so popular in the eighteenth century. The two upper panels are glazed to allow daylight to penetrate to the passage beyond.

century) made a considerable difference to cottage doors. Softwood and the development of machine techniques made possible the mass production of the four-panelled door. This feature probably came to the countryside via the builders' merchants who provided the materials for the Victorian expansion of our towns.

When a door led into an unlit passage the upper panels were often glazed. During the Georgian period a fanlight above the doorway became an accepted decoration and a way of providing light to an interior passage. Wood, lead, wrought or cast iron were used in fanlight construction. The latter material helped to blur the fading distinctions between town and countryside styles at the time of the Regency.

If an exterior door was capped with a rounded arch the space was sometimes filled with a lantern to provide a light for callers during darkness. A surprising number of these lanterns remain *in situ*. They were probably the work of the local blacksmith and although we might associate them with townlife their presence in a village setting helps to illustrate the way in which urban fashions slowly but surely invaded rural society. Towns may be subject to more changes than the village and the apparent survival of more lanterns in rural England could reflect this probability.

Englishmen have lavished a lot of attention on their front doors. Even when urban ideas were imported they were usually distilled by the local carpenter. The reality which emerged was the unmistakable quintessence of the rural craft tradition.

Another feature favoured in the eighteenth century was a door knocker shaped like a lion's head. There must be thousands of examples like this one. The design is still favoured and reproductions are obtainable. On an old door many coats of paint slowly mask the original detail and some ancient knockers could be improved by the removal of their encrusted accretions.

ABOVE LEFT

A pediment portico is a grand affair. This example has the rich dentil moulding which was a popular Georgian feature. The classical taper which adds to the apparent height of the columns is echoed by those formed on the wall. Next to the well-worn step we can see a vintage bootscraper which reminds us that in former years our village (and town) streets could be very muddy indeed.

ABOVE

Great skill was shown by eighteenth century craftsmen in the way they interpreted classical ideas. Our English climate makes it an advantage to have a door set deep into the wall. This Georgian doorcase has attracted later accretions in the shape of a Victorian knocker, a modern letterbox, a bellpush and a cylinder lock. The iron fence which originated in the village blacksmith's shop probably belongs to the latter part of Victoria's reign.

LEFT

Tradesmen did not call at the front door of the larger houses which followed the urban idea and possessed a tradesman's entrance. This door which leads to the rear of the building has few pretensions but it is still a much grander affair than most cottage doorways. The keystone has a modern 'roof'.

A high step protects the passageway from water which could otherwise creep in from the street. Notice the wedge-shaped bricks which are used to form the arch.

ABOVE

A doorway situated at the top of a flight of steps looks particularly imposing. This one with its semi-circular fan light and detailed tracery is probably a product of the Regency era. The railings with their circular panels complement the fanlight's features. Without looking at the doorknob we could guess which way the door opens by looking at the way the steps are worn. On the wall a tablet tells us that Gustav Holst lived here from 1917 to 1925.

ABOVE RIGHT

A door with a lantern.

RIGHT

Hawes, North Riding, Yorks: This Wensleydale doorway is typical of the fashion followed in the Pennines in the seventeenth century. The style and quality of the lettering tells us something about the hardness of the stone. Notice the inner door with its glazed panels. Tom Parker.

The Wind's Door

Now that all our primitive dwellings of the prehistoric period have more or less passed away – though there are some exceptions even today – we can easily disregard the way in which our modern windows actually evolved. It seems as if the dwellings used by our Norse and Anglo-Saxon ancestors were windowless – in the modern sense. If we look at the language of our forefathers we find that the Old Norse word 'wind-auga' meant wind-eye. The Anglo-Saxon 'wind-dur' simply meant the wind-door. Imagination will allow us to conjure up a picture of a house with a single hole in the wall which admitted both residents and daylight. When the hole was barred so was the light. Those who have noticed the villagers' preference to leave the front door open wide throughout most of the suitable summer days observe a habit unspeakably old and essentially practical in the era of its origin.

Later on a small peep hole in the wall – the wind's eye – was made. This was eventually provided with a shutter which could be removed entirely in daylight hours. Gradually the size of the peep hole increased. When it had become large enough to admit a prospective intruder bars were added which divided the space and made the premises secure. The removable shutter remained and it eventually became the basis for the frame which was 'glazed' with thin sheets of horn or, as an alternative, oiled cloth. These rudimentary windows were placed high up in the wall – a position which some people claim lessened the effect of internal draughts. Primitive windows of this kind are still to be found on the walls of old buildings. Some are glazed with a diamond-paned lattice, others are blocked and a few still retain their original bars.

Glass of a kind was made in England at least as long ago as the Saxon period, but this

precious commodity was then reserved for the Church and noblemen alone. Centuries elapsed before glass worked its way down the social strata and graced the artisan's home at some time late in the seventeenth century. The old windows with a diamond or rectangular array of panes were leaded together. Small fixed windows still survive and some of these may easily date from the seventeenth century. Glass, however, allowed the window to continue its development. There are disadvantages in having a fixed window as it did not help the smoke to escape. An anonymous genius provided the answer and invented the casement which opens on its hinges like the door itself. If part of the window could be made to open then the other half, or two thirds, could be fixed and was, therefore, more or less draughtproof. The three-light leaded casements which still grace so many of our cottages are probably no earlier than eighteenth century in origin. In Victorian times the leaded casement was

Not all walls are exactly flat and this one bends to suit a change in the direction of the village street. To avoid difficulties for the glazier the sills have been cut to suit the profile of the wall and two divisions (lights) are used instead of the usual three.

often replaced by a wooden frame which could hold large panes of glass.

Seventeenth-century gentlemen were able to indulge in the extravagance of the vertical sash windows with their larger panes. Eventually this status symbol made its way down the social ladder too until, in the nineteenth century, even modest dwellings possessed sashes.

In a no-man's-land of its own there is yet another type of window which is half-sash and half-casement. The part which opens slides in a horizontal groove. Different observers seem to use alternative names for windows of this intermediate type. It is not so very easy to place the sliding casement in an exact period of time. The idea of a sliding shutter to cover the wind's eye is, however, probably older than the seventeenth century. Quite large buildings will be found to possess sliding casements, eg brew houses, windmills, farmhouses, as well as ordinary cottages. For some odd reason which eludes the author the largest sliding casements always seem to contain the smallest panes.

Such was the progress of the industrial revolution that it eventually turned its attention to architecture and the mass-produced, cast-iron window frame was born. It too has an abundance of small panes. Iron windows usually follow the old casement style.

The need to keep out unwanted intruders remained a problem even in the nineteenth century. An external shutter which also served to protect the glass provided a suitable answer. During daylight the hinged shutters were opened and secured with an iron turn-button fixed to the wall. Long after the original shutters have gone these fragments of ironwork often remain. Migrant townsmen who 'do up' country cottages frequently make the mistake of 'restoring' shutters on both ground and upper floors! The purpose of the shutter was to protect and its use was usually peculiar to the ground floor. This is why an old shutter will be found to have a peep hole somewhere in the middle – to spy danger lurking without. Such a device, of course, takes us right back to the beginning when windows were merely the 'wind's eye'.

Some windows still have their shutters and the catches to retain them.

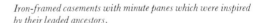

Iron-framed casements with minute panes which were inspired by their leaded ancestors.

ABOVE
Arthington, West Riding, Yorks: Nunnery House in Wharfe-dale is a house of many windows. In the days of the window tax a number were blocked up and remain as blind windows today. Arthur Gaunt FRGS.

LEFT
A sliding sash window. Sometimes called a sliding casement.

Sundials

The first sundials were probably made in ancient Babylon and Egypt. Cleopatra's Needle (1475 BC) which stands by the Thames in London may have been part of an Egyptian sun clock. Greeks and Romans both made use of sundials and it was probably the latter who erected the first dials in these islands. Our oldest dials were fashioned long after the Romans went home. The mass dials which can be found on some parish churches marked the tides – or times – of the monastic services. Eventually mechanical clocks replaced the sundial, but it remained a fashionable architectural decoration. Some of the domestic dials to be seen today date from the seventeenth or eighteenth centuries. Like so many other objects which include inscriptions the style of lettering, and the sentiments of the motto, can provide us with a clue to a dial's period of origin. A good many dials bear both Latin and English inscriptions.

There are two common types of dial to be seen. Horizontal dials are situated on low pillars; and the second type, probably more numerous, appear on vertical walls. Fewer in number, but not in interest, are the circular dials which often hide in secluded gardens.

Sundials have a peculiar individual quality. They indicate a 'local time' which once determined the pattern of local affairs. When you stop to think about it the sun appears to move round the earth at 15 degrees an hour. Noon in London is about twenty minutes ahead of noon at Newquay (Cornwall) which is some five degrees further west. Such differences were of little importance in stage-coach days, but the coming of the railways helped to make local time obsolete.

England has an abundance of dials with interesting features or associations. There is a touch of irony in the fact that the railway pioneer George Stephenson made a sundial to go over his cottage door at Killingworth, Northumberland (c1815) when that place was still a mining village. What is probably the largest dial in the land can be seen at Seaton Ross, Yorks. It is about 120 years old and spreads its diameter of twelve feet, across a cottage wall. The dial was created by a local farmer, William Watson.

Wherever you go in England there are dials to be seen. According to the late A. P. Herbert people who study sundials are 'skiaphilists' (shadow lovers). Essential reading for those who pursue the fascination is A. P. Herbert's *Sundials Old and New* (1967).

Not all dials greet the rising sun. If a house faces west no dial can register the morning hours. This one counts the hours which follow noon and so the plain style is set slantwise. The left-hand side of the dial protrudes from the wall to allow the instrument to be correctly aligned.

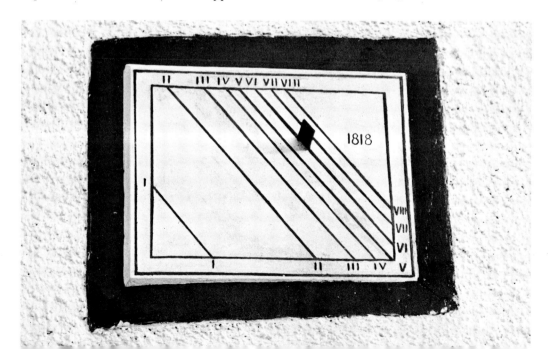

Maude Heath's Causeway, East Tytherton, Wilts: The dreadful state of our roads in past ages led some men and women to remember us mortal travellers in their wills. This splendid sundial, which was erected over two centuries after the original bequest, provides us, however, with some insight into seventeenth-century thought and design.

A closer view of the dial. The right-hand face looks southwards and so it has a gnomon set in a vertical plane. It records the morning and afternoon hours but its fellow (left) begins to count at two. For some curious reason best known to the mason the hours from 9.30 am until 2.30pm are divided into quarters. Notice the bell-shaped gnomon on the left and the manner in which the lines on this dial are inscribed. The erection of a dial provided an opportunity to add a pithy moral maxim. Those recorded here are in Latin and English. Hence we read above the southern face – 'Quin Tempus Habemu Operemur Bonum' (While we have time let us do good) and below 'Life Steals away this hour Oh Man is Lent thee Patiently work the work of Him who sent thee'. On the western dial we read 'Redibo Tu nunquam' (I will never return) and 'Haste Traveller the Sun is sinking now He shall return again but never thou'.

Henbury, Glos: Blaise Castle Hamlet was built (1811) to provide a home for retired servants from Blaise Castle. John Nash was the architect of the ten cottages which cluster round a green. The porches are so arranged that no doorway over- *looks another. A feature of special visual interest is the sundial-cum-weathervane-cum-pump shown here. Water emerges from the lion's mouth. Clive Street.*

37

ABOVE LEFT
Madeley, Shropshire: This curious sundial at Madeley Court dates from the days of Elizabeth I. Its features include a series of holes which pass through the block. They were used to determine the positions of the planets and the moon. Frank Rodgers.

ABOVE
Brougham, Westmorland: A memorial which marks the place where the Lady Anne Clifford finally parted from her daughter. The 'Countess's Pillar' was erected in 1656. A gnomon is now missing from the central dial. Tom Parker.

LEFT
Sydenham, Oxon: This redundant dial now serves as a keyhole.

Murals and Inscriptions

For a very long time walls have attracted various kinds of decorations. Englishmen seem to have taken delight in writing on their walls or adding to them curious embellishments. A common but unwritten principle seems to apply to our walls. Unlike Newton's Law of Gravity what goes up seldom, if ever, comes down! This reluctance to interfere with the accretions of the past is usually to be applauded. A walk down almost any village street will reveal something of interest which has been left behind. The mere fact that objects have occupied the same place for decade after decade often has the effect of making them 'invisible' to those who pass them almost every day. We so often miss the obvious simply because it lies above our normal eye level and becomes merged into the anonymous expanse of our half-seen surroundings.

Mural decorations are not always part of the original structure. A high proportion have been added for one reason or another during the course of time. It is not always an easy matter to trace the origin of decorative features. When the old monasteries were dissolved by Henry VIII many of them became quarries for local builders. The habit of 'borrowing' from empty or derelict habitations is not new.

Where initials or dates survive they help to point to the identity of former owners and the time of construction or rebuilding. Information of this kind can mislead. A date on a porch may refer only to its erection and the actual fabric of the house could be considerably older.

Whatever remains can inform or puzzle us. A good deal of forgotten information probably still lurks behind the ivy on many an old building. The subject is not exhausted by the examples presented here.

ABOVE

This plaster figure can now be seen decorating a Wiltshire house, but it probably came from a mansion of some importance when the latter was demolished or altered. Such things get passed down – like old clothes! There can be no doubt that classical ideas determined the posture of the maiden.

RIGHT

In the eighteenth century it was fashionable to enhance a large house with romantic or heroic figures and groups. This helmeted damsel appears to be a goddess of some sort. Her missing left hand probably held an emblem which would have helped identification.

39

ABOVE

This eighteenth-century view of woodcutters is attached to a modest cottage.

ABOVE

A cast-iron head with classical features from Staffordshire.

BELOW

Even a modest cottage can sometimes present us with a detail of particular interest. This elegant cartouche is formed from moulded bricks. The plaster decoration within is fashioned on finely textured and close-jointed bricks which contrast dramatically with the remainder of the wall. Initials can often leave us with a puzzle to solve, but these probably belong to Nicholas Bent who seems to have owned the property in the late seventeenth century.

BELOW

In the limestone belt inscriptions are often carved on stone tablets. Where a date is provided we can assign the style of the lettering employed to a definite period. The study of lettering is a subject with a fascination of its own. Much will depend on the material as well as the time of origin. Where two sets of initials appear on the same tablet the builder as well as the owner may be indicated.

Charlton, Herts: A date cannot always be taken literally and this example obviously originated long after the year cited. The practice of providing buildings with a tablet of this kind can add much to our appreciation of the surroundings. They would also serve to show that a considerable part of the nation's talent had its origin in the countryside. Henry Bessemer is probably best remembered for the steel smelting process he invented.

Stone and flint go well together. If the flint is knapped to expose its darker core it can provide an interesting contrast. This panel records the year of origin and two sets of initials. An old directory tells us that there was a J.P. (James Plested) in the parish at the time. He was a wheelwright and familiar with the tradition which allowed him to paint his name on the rear end of the vehicles he made or repaired. We may guess that H.I. was the builder. Letters and figures here are made from more or less uniform blocks and this to some extent determines their shapes.

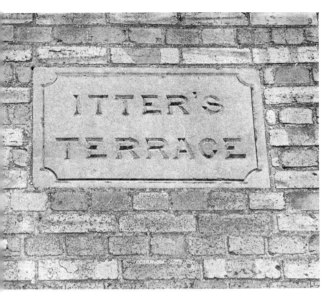

ABOVE
Towards the end of the last century lettering of this kind was influenced by the printed word of the newspaper and advertising. The inspiration of the country stone mason began to wane and more stereotyped letter forms gained acceptance. This simple tablet provides us with an example of this trend towards uniformity. Even a modest inscription of this variety is useful. Here we can read the name of a country brickmaker. When he built a terrace of cottages for his workmen he was modest enough to name it after himself.

BELOW
Inscriptions carved in wood do not often survive in an external situation. These two panels from the posts of a barn door

provide us with an example of seventeenth-century lettering.

ABOVE
Aphorisms too seem to have a place on some buildings. This tablet incorporates the name of the dwelling as well.

RIGHT
Didmarton, Glos: A collection of bygones adds interest to a blank wall. Among these quaint and curious objects we can see a breast plough (top centre); a roller scotch and a drug bat – used on wagons to prevent them running away on steep slopes; a cast-iron pump; a trough; and a wooden bell wheel. Clive Street.

Weathervanes

Long before Shakespeare mentioned 'the vane on the house' (*Much Ado About Nothing*), Englishmen were quite used to weathervanes creaking on their rooftops. As a nation we seem to have a passionate interest in knowing which way the wind blows. There is an ancient tradition which attributes the origin of our windvanes to a papal decree, made in Saxon times, which commanded the erection of vanes on all churches. Perhaps this is why the weathercock became so popular since it had a particular significance for Christians. The most ancient vane in the land seems to be the cock which sits on the spire at Ottery St Mary, Devon. It can also blow its own trumpet as there are two cone-shaped tubes passing through its body, which produce a musical note when the wind is strong enough. This bird has been watching our weather since the fourteenth century – so it is said.

Some vanes portray local legends. The vane at Crab Farm, Shapwich, Dorset, shows a man being carried in a wheelbarrow to see a crab. Local tradition insists that a travelling fishmonger once dropped a crab in the village when he was on his rounds. Villagers, unable to identify the creature, are supposed to have brought the oldest inhabitant in a barrow to see the mystery for himself.

Most windvanes were the work of the local blacksmith and it is sometimes possible to identify a common likeness among vanes which probably reflect one craftsman's personal style.

Weathervanes are not simply bygones and each year country blacksmiths provide discerning owners with vanes of their own. Several of those shown below are modern in origin. A vane can tell us a good deal about the householder's interests. One kind of vane user – the farmer – has more predictable tastes. Cows, bulls, horses and pigs seem to dominate the agricultural scene.

TOP LEFT
Several vanes have been inspired by the imaginary world of heraldic beasts. This gryphon – half lion and half eagle – is a useful shape to catch the wind.

LEFT
This vane is shaped like a flag and bears a proud owner's initials. It probably dates from the eighteenth century. The pointer has a decorative end which complements the swirling edge of the flag itself.

RIGHT
The addition of a date is sometimes helpful, but we must not assume that it always tells us the age of the building. Such information is usually a more reliable guide to the antiquity of the vane.

ABOVE
Some modern vanes have a humorous touch like this cock and snail.

ABOVE RIGHT
An appropriate vane for a smithy. While the patient horse waits, the blacksmith prepares a shoe.

A modern reminder of the wild life which once roamed freely in medieval England.

The technique of using cast aluminium allows more detail to be obtained. You can almost count the feathers on these elegant ducks.

Man's first servant.

Ironwork

The blacksmith was a craftsman who enjoyed a special place in village life. From childhood onwards there was a particular importance in the wonders which he forged from the blinding whiteness of his fire. The wide-eyed child who waited, with a sticky sixpence in his hand, for the magic welding of an iron hoop would return years later with a horse for shoeing or a broken harrow to be mended.

Our early clocks were the product of the blacksmith's shop. His craft called for all kinds of knowledge which was hidden from other men. Anyone who doubts the blacksmith's mastery of mathematics should consider the clock on page 77.

To make and mend was part of the smith's daily round. Many a cottage has been saved from collapse by the use of a few well-placed tie bars, which hold sagging brickwork together for years on end.

No task was too difficult for the smith. When cast iron came into use he mastered its principles and added iron-founding to his list of skills. Sometimes we can find the smith's name on the things he manufactured, but all too often we are left to guess their origin. Space will allow only a few examples to be included here. The reader who really looks for himself will find many more.

All kinds of history has been left hanging around and one should not be surprised to find even a penny farthing (which fortunately does not have a decimal equivalent) employed as a decoration. Since this photograph was taken this antiquity of transport history has been taken indoors – where the elements cannot rust it away so fast. Before the invasion of the motor car, cycling was an idyllic form of getting about but to control a machine of this type needed a sound constitution, courage and skill.

47

Examples of the blacksmith's work crept into practically every home in the village. He made tools for the farmer and for himself. This crane came from the forge upon which it still hangs. It also served as a splendid trade sign although it had a specific usefulness to its owner.

One of the blacksmith's skills was his ability to produce cast-iron objects. From the eighteenth century onwards there was an unabated demand for objects made from this material. We are inclined to think that all such things came only from industrial towns, but there were hundreds of small foundries in the countryside. This splendid lamp bracket with its flowing involutes probably dates from the early eighteenth century. The stays and lamp holder are made of wrought iron. Too many treasures of this sort went into the melting pot in 1939.

The demand for cast- or wrought-iron gates and fences did not vanish until this century. Cast iron was usually favoured for the gatepost and, depending upon expense sometimes also for the rails. Gates, usually, seem to have been made from wrought iron – a factor which helped reduce the weight. This example, however, combines a wrought-iron frame and the most agreeable cast acorns. Gateposts provided the best opportunity for the maker to add his name – 'W. T. Loveday Maker Aldbourne'.

Cast posts with wrought-iron gate and fence. The design is simple with its traditional double hoops. Patterns did not change a great deal and identical gates came from the same forge in Jubilee year (1887) and half a century later. The task of making the wooden patterns from which the mould was prepared was no doubt carried out by the village carpenter. Blacksmiths and carpenters were accustomed to complementing one another as so many jobs about the village demanded both skills.

ABOVE LEFT

The simplest way of keeping a door shut from within was to place a bar across its width – hence the expression 'barr the door'. In the old days few villagers bothered to secure their dwellings even at night. Each villager knew everyone else and most had nothing worth stealing nor a distrust of the neighbours. The first locks were used on buildings of importance like the manor house and the church. From the nineteenth century onwards locks and keys gradually worked down the social scale until the most humble dwellings had a keyhole, at least on the front door. Early keys are usually robust and large. A good many old cottages have keys like this still in daily use.

ABOVE RIGHT

Brickwork and stone can begin to bulge outwards with the passage of time. To prevent a wall collapsing the village blacksmith was engaged to make a tie bar. This was a simple device consisting of a rod and two bars. A hole was made in the offending wall and the two bars – one on the inside – were joined together with the rod. The threaded end allowed the nut to be tightened and the wall gripped like a vice. Tie bars vary in size and design but this one has a particular interest. The ends of the 'S' are shaped with a mouth. An 'eye' is also punched to give each extremity a 'snake's head'. This device has a special and ancient significance. As long ago as the Bronze Age (c2000 BC) the two-headed sun snake was a symbol of considerable religious significance. It is not easy to explain why or how the design endured through the centuries. There was an enormous gap in time when there was no demand for tie bars in any case. Nevertheless there are probably many hundreds of sun snakes – emblem of the pagan Sun God – still 'protecting' unsuspecting villagers.

CENTRE LEFT
A design from Sussex.

BOTTOM LEFT
This Hampshire serpent has a forked tail.

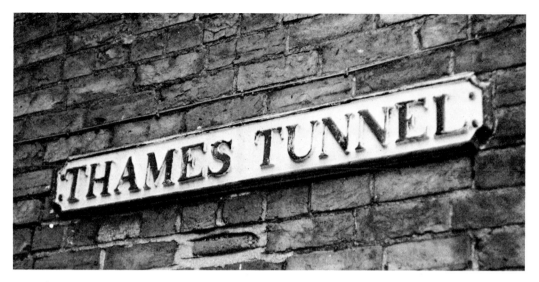

TOP

Lettering on cast-iron plates usually reflects the contemporary taste. The names employed here, however, are just as interesting as the lettering. Not only is the Thames over a hundred miles away, but the tunnel is simply an alleyway. To track down the origin of curious names is frequently very difficult. Long usage wraps their invention in total obscurity. They form part of an oral tradition which was seldom written down.

CENTRE

Cast iron had many different uses and it has proved to be a very durable material. In some of our larger villages, streets and passageways were given visible names in Victorian days. It is part of the village tradition to attach personal names to fields, houses, lanes and pathways. The name given here probably belonged to a shopkeeper.

The English seem very reluctant to remove anything once it has been erected. If you leave something long enough, of course, it is bound to become numbered among the bygones. White helmeted wardens probably turned their headwear into flowerpots, but the nameplates they had to display frequently remain in situ.

Wells and Pumps

Today we turn on the tap and take running water for granted but the luxury of water indoors is not so very old in many country places. A water supply is a basic domestic need and it was a factor which determined the site of many village settlements in the dim and distant past. No doubt in the very beginning there was a single village well. Over the centuries new ones were made, starting with the lord of the manor's personal well, until even humble dwellings had a supply quite close at hand.

The old style pumps were made from an immense block of elm – a wood which will withstand the wet. To bore a hole exactly through the length of an elm pump called for considerable skill. Our admiration for the craftsmen who made them is enhanced when we consider that all the work involved was performed without the aid of powered machines. Care, patience and dexterity were essential qualities for a village carpenter to possess. Ironwork for the wooden pump was provided by the village blacksmith. A great revolution took place when cast iron was employed for pump making. Cast iron meant mass production and the cost of a pump gradually declined.

The pinnacle of status for ordinary villagers was reached when it became possible to have a pump fitted indoors. This Utopian arrangement avoided the wearisome business of going outside to unfreeze the pump on a winter's morning, just because you had forgotten to draw off a bucket or two the night before. This advanced style of plumbing was not universal of course. Most farmworkers were still going outside for their water in the 1920s.

It is quite surprising to find just how many pumps of both kinds remain. Some, like the splendid example at Aldbourne, Wilts, still work; much to the surprise of those who are tempted to operate the handle! A pump can be an attractive village feature and wherever possible such things should be preserved. There are still many examples of shared pumps to be seen. When the Victorian terrace invaded the village a single pump was usually provided in a prominent position for the residents to share.

Pumps and wells co-existed until the coming of the mains supply. Those who knew the crystal coolness of real well water will testify to its superiority.

Thames Valley: A stout wooden frame supports the winding gear and the roof of this village well-head. Piped water indoors has made its original purpose obsolete and the trapdoor is padlocked for safety. When a part of our past is cared for like this, it cannot fail to add to the interest of the village scene.

ABOVE

Stoke Row, Oxon: The magnificent well presented to this hill-top village by the Maharajah of Benares in 1864. Although the canopy has definite Indian features the actual winding gear was supplied by Messrs Wilder of Wallingford. Those who visit can buy a short history of the structure from the shop across the road.

ABOVE RIGHT

Stoke Row, Oxon: The octagonal well head was cared for by the well keeper who lived in this hexagonal cottage.

RIGHT

Bedfordshire: Water on tap, but the tap is still out of doors. There is a shelf to hold the bucket. The designer could not forget the Classical Revival and so we see a dome and a lion's head.

53

Tissington, Derbyshire: One of the joys of the Derbyshire summer is the reverence which is still shown for the custom of well dressing. Here we see the parable of the Good Samaritan beautifully portrayed in flowers, mosses and other natural materials which have been pressed into flat panels of clay. The custom is also observed at Youlgrave, Ashford-in-the-Water and Wirksworth. Arthur Gaunt FRGS

An example with a wooden case, lead spout and an iron handle. A pump of this kind would have been made by village craftsmen and it is for this reason that we can find such a variety of designs.

A pump with two spouts – one above the trough and the other high up to suit the needs of a steam engine. Notice the way in which the long spout is supported. Both the pump handles are missing.

ABOVE
During the nineteenth century many village wells were improved by the addition of a pump. Many cast-iron pumps followed the pattern of the wooden kind and had a handle at the side.

ABOVE RIGHT
Pumps of this type, with an overhead drive, have quite a different visual impact. The bowl to catch the spillage is supported on a rough limestone plinth.

RIGHT
A few pumps seem to have been inspired by Gothic architecture. This splendid octagonal column had a row of lancet arches and an ogee cap. The handle has lost its pivot, but a padlock and chain has prevented it from wandering. Such an essay in cast iron deserves to be more than a post for a litter basket. In the background we can glimpse some cobbles which were so common in Victoria's time.

LEFT
Another example with a wooden case. The spout is supported by a wrought-iron bracket.

BELOW
A lead rainwater head which has been re-used and now forms a junction between two downpipes. The ornamentation is detailed and well executed.

Shops

We are used to the idea of old shops in towns, but our view of rural commerce is perhaps less well informed. Following the great exodus from the land, when the gentry enclosed the common fields in the eighteenth century, there were great changes in the structure and conduct of village affairs. No doubt there were shops of a kind to be found in our villages before the enclosures. It seems likely that the retailer conducted his business without the help of a recognisable shopfront. When a village was organised on more or less feudal lines there was probably little need to attract customers. They all knew where the retailer lived. As things changed and more and more travellers appeared on the roads, there was some advantage in copying the fashion of the town in order to attract passing trade. The urban shopkeeper knew all about the advantages of a conspicuous shop front. When this latter innovation was introduced into the village the urban style set the pattern. The village shop played an important part in village life from the eighteenth cen-

tury onwards. Until the omnibus invaded the countryside in the 1930s the village shopkeeper had little competition from outside his immediate community. Larger villages were often able to support several shops.

As long ago as the 1850s a considerable range of retail trades was represented in certain villages. All the usual trades seem to have been present – butcher, baker, grocer, draper, brewer, beer retailer, corn and coal dealer, harness maker, tailor, shoemaker, haberdasher, currier, rope maker, confectioner, tobacconist, milliner, greengrocer, fruiterer, chemist, dairyman, tea dealer and stay maker. There was also the fellmonger who dealt in hides, and the tallow chandler. The latter owed his title to the Old French word 'chandelier' which conjures up visions of rich candle-lit ballrooms. Tallow chandlers provided candles, oil, soap, paint and groceries. In the long years before electricity came – on its hideous poles – our cottages were lit with the gentle light of candles or oil from the tallow chandlers' stores.

The features of the village shop window will depend upon its date of origin. We can probably distinguish three distinct kinds of window which have survived in our villages. Some may date from the Georgian period and have a flat picture-frame shape divided by small panes which shelter below an equally

Kimbolton, Hunts: A quiet corner where a variety of window styles meet together. Notice the cobbles favoured by our ancestors.

58

flat cornice. This style seems to have been followed by the delightful bow-shape to which we usually attach the Regency label. When it became possible to manufacture larger panes of glass the flat window seems to have returned to favour but it now had bigger 'eyes'. The eighteenth-century shop may still have its six-panelled door, but the Victorian age seems to have favoured the curious stable-door style which was cut across the middle. This allowed the upper half to remain open when the lower half was closed to guard against those draughts across the floor. There was another advantage in this arrangement. The shopkeeper had a view across the street and many a greeting must have echoed across those half-open portals during the course of a working day.

With the changes which have taken place in the village many shops have closed and become dwellings. Their shopfronts remain however. The 'shop' is now probably a sitting room which lies hidden from the gaze of passing villagers beyond a veil of nylon curtain. Another clue to help identify a former shop comes from a glance at its doorstep. It may bear evidence of the thousands of feet which have worn its surface into a deep concave. Village carpenters no doubt created most of our rural shopfronts and this is why each one has characteristics peculiar to itself.

ABOVE
Kinver, Staffs: A modest shopfront with a private door to the domestic quarters.

BELOW
Thaxted, Essex: The village shop was an important institution in the last century. Quite ordinary cottages were used as shops, but eventually the townsman's idea of a shop began to influence village shopkeepers. The oldest village shopfronts seem to have their origins in the eighteenth century. The two shown here provide us with a contrast in styles. Bow-shaped windows were in favour during the Georgian period, but the larger panes of the right-hand example suggest a later origin.

ABOVE

Aldbourne, Wilts: Sometimes the size of the shopfront provided the carpenter with special problems. To attract trade the largest possible window was required, but a doorway also had to be squeezed in to allow the customers to enter. Part of the shopkeeper's living room window was sacrificed in this example and the casement has been reduced to two lights. The base of the coloured stone and brick walls has been tarred to help keep out the rising damp.

LEFT

Wendover, Bucks: A shopfront from the nineteenth century. Notice the double door.

ABOVE RIGHT

Watlington, Oxon: An eighteenth-century shopfront which is probably the most outstanding example to be found in any English village. The double shop door is on the left. The other provided access to the private apartments. Surviving Victorian lettering tells us that this was a tallow chandler's premises.

RIGHT

Selborne, Hants: Gilbert White planted the trees outside this butcher's shop, to 'hide the blood', in the eighteenth century.

3
The Great House

There was a time in Saxon and Norman England when the lord of the manor shared a great hall with his retainers. At least this is the popular picture of those distant days. Even the robust stone keep of the Norman era had a hall which was surrounded by private quarters formed in the thickness of the massive walls. Gradually, as the monarch's power strengthened to the point where private wars between the barons ceased, the need for a fortified house diminished. At this stage the shape of the feudal lord's dwelling began to change. For a long time the hall remained the central feature of lordly living. Private rooms were eventually positioned in a separate wing of their own. In the Middle Ages the lord's kitchen was, it seems, a building detached from the main hall altogether. Examples of such structures still survive at Stanton Harcourt, Oxon, and Glastonbury, Somerset. This arrangement may have kept kitchen smells away from the living quarters, but the dinner's long procession to the lord's table must have affected its temperature. As society's fashions changed the lord withdrew to a private dining room and left his steward to commune with the servants of the household.

The habits of the manorial lords had an effect on the household arrangements of the lesser gentry who usually copied their social conventions. During the Middle Ages the expanding ranks of well-off wool merchants added to our architectural heritage by building new houses suited to their business and domestic needs. As the status of the older gentry changed, their original hall-houses were discarded and they built fashionable houses on a larger scale than the merchant's home. Rank alone contributed to the trend. One-upmanship is not a new phenomenon on the social scene. Once the ancient halls were abandoned – no doubt at a good price! – farmers or members of the merchant classes moved in. Their need for a great hall was not so strong. As fashions favoured smaller rooms each with specific functions the old halls were divided. When smoke-holes in the roof were replaced with a chimney stack and a fireplace in the wall, it became possible to construct an upper floor below a hall's high roof. Gradually plastered ceilings too were added for comfort and in this way many a handsome roof truss has been hidden away – and totally forgotten.

Tattershall Castle, Lincs: The lofty 112ft tower built by Ralph Cromwell, Lord High Treasurer to Henry VI, is the most magnificent example of early English brickwork (c1434–48). Some 322,000 bricks were used in its construction. They were made at Edlington Moor less than ten miles distant. Although the tower follows the shape of the Norman keep it was not intended to be defended. The windows, with their dressings of Ancaster stone, also bear witness to those less troubled days. A National Trust property – not to be missed!

As England's fortunes changed and the fashions of society altered new ideas about architecture were borrowed from other lands. The Renaissance had a considerable effect on the homes of the gentry and in the eighteenth century classical ideas came into fashion. An Age of Reason demanded not only a great house but a considerable parkland to surround it. A century later the New Gothic style with its romantic turrets became the object of the gentleman's delight. There were more men of substance to follow fashion, of course, as the Industrial Revolution had made many a fortune. The story of the great house did not spill into the twentieth century. A war of nations (1914–1918) had a profound impact on our society. The carnage of the trenches left few to return and labour on country estates. Male heirs too went to war never to return. Old orders which depended upon descendants could never replace the missing links in the chain of succession. Great houses lost both sons and servants. Their cavernous interiors were costly to maintain in a climate of a steady inflation. Slowly the gentry retreated and one by one country seats were exchanged for more modest surroundings. The buildings themselves were sometimes demolished. Others were bequeathed to the nation. Those which remained often became schools or served some other institutional purpose.

It seems unlikely that any great houses will be built on such a grand scale in England again. We may view with displeasure the social systems which fostered their creation, but who can fail to appreciate the superb proportions they display; or admire a prospect Capability Brown could see only in his mind's eye when workmen planted the saplings which now frame the landscape as glorious elms?

To walk the topiary set lawns of Compton Wynyates or watch swallows sweep below the immense bridge at Blenheim, all bathed in a summer sun, is to glimpse grandeur – a quality with a style of its own that even village shopkeepers delighted to echo in their doorways.

ABOVE
In 1911 Tattershall Castle was in a state of dereliction and it was on the point of being dismembered and taken across the Atlantic when Lord Curzon saved it for the nation. This is one of four chimney pieces which had, in fact, travelled as far as Tilbury Docks when they were recovered! What feastings this Ancaster stone has seen we can only imagine. The excellence of its heraldic decoration, however, is as rich as its former master's venison.

BELOW
A detail of the heraldry. Alternate panels show the same design – a purse suspended from two interlaced branches. This is, of course, a symbol of Ralph Cromwell's office.

Stowe, Bucks: In the eighteenth century classical ideas pre-dominated in English architecture. Gentlemen followed fashion and the age of great parks laid out in a 'natural style' began. The straight lines of Tudor gardening with its rigid symmetry were discarded. Capability Brown's name is widely known. He was in charge of the gardens at Stowe early in his career. This view shows the south façade overlooking the Octagon Lake which was an octagon until it had its edges smudged in the 1730s.

Stowe's importance today arises from the fact that it did not suffer from Victorian innovations. The eighteenth-century atmosphere survives and this distinguishes it from so many other great houses. One of the delights of Stowe is its unequalled wealth of garden temples. They are the work of various designers. This bust, however, comes from The Temple of British Worthies, the work of William Kent c1735.

This Gothic Temple was designed by James Gibbs and dates from the 1740s. It marks the dawning of the Neo-Gothic era which endured until the end of Victoria's reign. The ironstone has weathered to a rusty pink. Triangular in plan, like the Lodge at Rushton, Northants, it has a tower at each corner. One of these, the tallest, has five sides.

The Rotondo was created by Vanbrugh in 1721 and modified by Borra some thirty years later. It once sheltered a statue of Venus. Ten Ionic pillars support the dome's classic proportions.

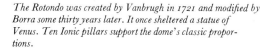

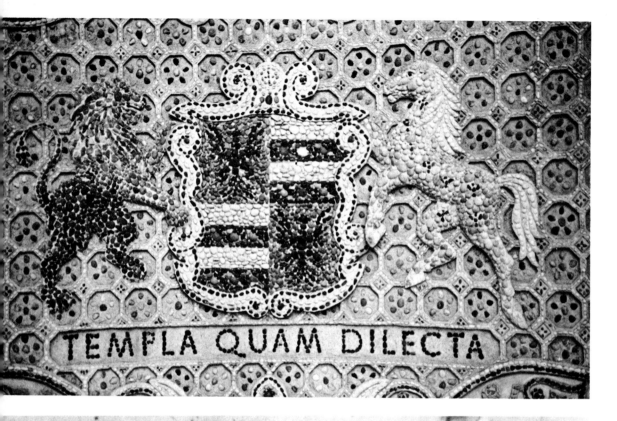

TEMPLA QUAM DILECTA

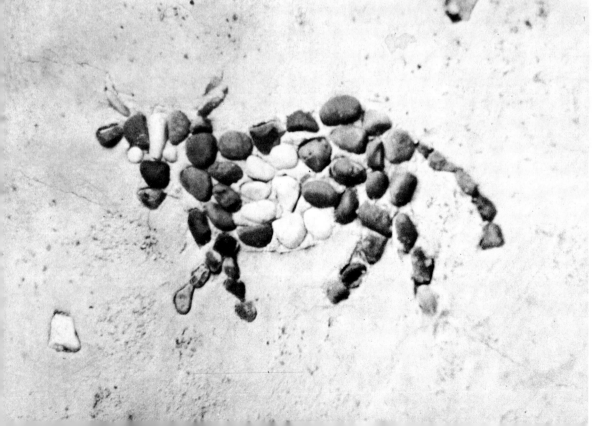

TOP LEFT

*A detail of the Pebble Alcove designed by William Kent. For
two centuries the fabric of the Pebble Alcove suffered from the
ravages of the elements. Its features were restored by Benjamin
Gibbon in 1967. The principal feature is Lord Cobham's arms.
He seems to have had a sense of humour if the family motto
below the shield is any guide 'Templa Quam Dilecta' (How
delightful are thy temples)!*

LEFT

*Benjamin Gibbon had a certain amount of void to decorate.
This allowed him to introduce the charm of a trotting
ruminant, other flora and some signs from the Zodiac.*

ABOVE

*The Palladian Bridge is Stowe's most splendid piece of garden
furniture. It was built c1742 and followed the lines of the
original set up at Wilton in Wiltshire. This bridge, however,
was designed for carriages as well as foot passengers. Unlike
Wilton's bridge there are richly ornamented keystones to be
seen here. Observed in the misty light of an autumn evening the
bridge seems to float in a world of its own. Superb proportions
and a perfect setting contribute much to such an illusion.*

RIGHT

*An interior view of the ceiling showing the lathes supporting
the plaster and the method of fixing the decorative foliage.*

Blenheim, Oxon: Vanbrugh's bridge c1710 with 100ft span to nowhere across the lake set out by Capability Brown. Today it is a matter of amazement for us to think that anyone could erect anything so ostentatious just for fun.

BELOW LEFT
Belvoir Castle, Leics: There has been a castle here since Norman times, but this building is a mixture of medieval and Victorian inspiration. The round tower may remind some readers of Windsor. Long ago the Englishman's castle was designed to keep unwanted visitors out. Now that so many of them have become stately homes that intention has been reversed.

ABOVE
Hertfordshire: A timber house of some importance with a later covering of plaster. One indication that this was the dwelling of a man of status comes from the splendid group of brick chimneys which are set arris-wise. The composition is given a final touch of distinction by the attractive topiary.

RIGHT
Wendover, Bucks: When a house had to jostle with its neighbours there were limitations to the way it could be 'improved'. A good many timber-framed houses hide behind an eighteenth-century façade of brick like this one. The cluster of chimney shafts also helps to give away the building's true identity.

Gates

ABOVE LEFT

*Shirburn, Oxon: A long-disused gateway in the Early English
style. The gatekeeper's cottage which included the tower has
one dormer window and a shuttered bay on the ground floor.
Iron spikes decorate and protect the decayed gates which are
slowly being enveloped by nature's advancing tide.*

BELOW LEFT

*Great Hampden, Bucks: These two octagonal gatehouses are
known as the 'Pepperpots'. They were built in the seventeenth
century and stand at the bottom of a long drive which leads to
John Hampden's house. About a century ago a gatekeeper
lived here with his family of eight children.*

ABOVE

*Once an estate is divided some entrances become obsolete and
with the passage of the years forgotten and overgrown.*

RIGHT

A gatepost with an armorial head.

4
Faith, Hope and Charity

The Church

Apart from its religious significance the village church once played an important part in the social life of the community. In times of danger the building could be a place of safety. This was perhaps less true in the seventeenth century when Parliament was at war with the King and some churches, so we are told, became stables or barracks for Roundhead soldiers. Most village churches have grown from small beginnings and their various additions provide us with a variety of architectural fashions. Almost every century seems to have made its contribution to fabric or furnishings. There are a few churches, however, which seem to have escaped extensive alterations, eg Stewkley, Bucks and Fairford, Glos. Like houses our churches reflect the geological characteristics of their neighbourhood. The result is an unending number of variations on the same theme. No two

churches are ever alike and until you have visited them all there is always something new to discover.

Churches which occupy hill-top sites are sometimes said to be built on Pagan places of worship. The possibility exists, but proof is usually another matter. We can be sure, however, that the churchyard shelters many generations of our ancestors. Medieval memorials to ordinary people do not exist. If they ever did perhaps they were made of wood like the weathered graveboards which have survived for a hundred years or so. From the seventeenth century onwards farmers, merchants, and the lesser gentry followed fashion and had their status marked by the erection of memorials in the churchyard. Lords and ladies qualified for a tomb in the church itself. Out of doors there appears to have been an acknowledged order of precedence which can sometimes be seen in the manner memorials are dispensed. The same system applied indoors each Sunday when quick men of substance occupied the pews at the front and lesser folk took a back seat. A churchyard can tell us a good deal about a village's former social hierarchy.

The exterior of the church can provide us with many clues to its development. Portions which have been added occasionally bear a date. Long ago when it was fashionable to go on pilgrimages to Canterbury, or even

Jerusalem, travellers often left a sign behind when they stopped to pray *en route*. These small votive crosses can usually be found in the stonework surrounding doorways. We do not know the names of these travellers, but each cross speaks of an individual penance which the temporal world has long forgotten. Individuality is the very essence of our country churches. The craftsmen who built the church or repaired it knew nothing of mass production. Each lintel, panel, bracket or bench-end deserved and received individual attention.

The Churchyard

BELOW LEFT
Fairford, Glos: A view of the churchyard which shows how close to it the village has crept. We can see from the buildings, roofs and monuments that this is stone country. Even here social distinctions are not lost. Simple headstones abound, but the slabs and table tombs are fewer in number. On the exterior wall of the church there are mural tablets – some well worn by time.

RIGHT
Long Compton, Warwicks: To enter this churchyard of well-shaped yews the visitor must pass beneath the thatched loft over the gateway. The room itself is a mixture of stone, half-timber and brick nogg. The chimney on the left suggests that the room may once have been used to house a priest.

BELOW
East Bergholt, Suffolk: The wooden belfry (or bell cage) which stands at the edge of the churchyard.

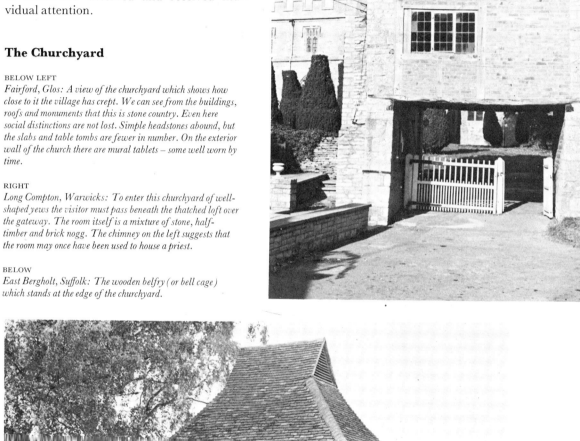

73

LEFT
Sutton Courtenay, Berks: A porch with a room above which was used, so it has been said, to provide shelter for a visiting priest. The chimney (left) tells us that there must be a fireplace within.

ABOVE
Weston-Turville, Bucks: A curious revolving gate which is controlled by a weight suspended on a chain which runs over two pulley wheels. Similar designs can be seen at Chalfont St Giles, Bucks, and Burnsall, West Riding, Yorks.

BELOW
Ewelme, Oxon: Above the flint and stone squares we can see a consecration cross – made by the bishop. It served a similar purpose to the amulets shown on page 50.

RIGHT
Bewcastle, Cumberland: An ancient Celtic cross with characteristic interlaced carving. The upper part of the shaft bears a semi-circular mass dial but the gnomon is missing. Tom Parker

RIGHT
*Eyam, Derbyshire: The Saxon cross which dates from the
ninth century.* Frank Rodgers

76

Dials

The oldest dials are usually to be found on our parish churches. Most have been eroded by the elements and their gnomons lost. This example is no more than a few scratches in the limestone. The large crater surrounding the hole shows us how the rusting gnomon caused the stonework to decay.

RIGHT
A relatively modern dial of the horizontal type. The shadow shows us the shape of the gnomon.

Our earliest clocks indicated the hours by striking a bell. When dials were first introduced they had a single hand. There were four divisions between each numeral to distinguish the quarters.

77

Clocks

Visitors to main line termini in London or to airports will be familiar with the new fashion for clocks without hands. Our very first mechanical clocks were handless too. They simply rang a bell to mark the passage of the hours. The word clock, in fact, comes from a Latin word meaning bell. Historians tell us that the Chinese invented the first clock mechanisms – about three thousand and a few hundred years ago. Europe, and England waited until the fourteenth century AD before reliable clocks appeared in our part of the globe.

One problem which early clockmakers had to overcome was to find some form of power to drive the clock mechanism. Gravity came to the rescue and heavy weights were attached to clocks. Ropes or chains supporting the weights were wound round a cylinder mounted on a spindle. As the weight slowly descended the barrel rotated and provided motion for the clock's system of gears. To prevent the weight dropping with a rush the speed of the mechanism was controlled by an escapement. It is a clock's escapement which provides us with the characteristic 'tick'. The mechanism which operated the striking gear was also driven by a suspended weight. Horologists call each system of gears 'a train'.

The early clocks usually had a 'going' and a 'striking' train and therefore required two weights to provide the necessary power. There are exceptions to most things of course. The clock at East Hendred, Berks, has three trains (see C. F. Beeson op. cit.). It is curious but true to say that these primitive timepieces were usually made by village blacksmiths. We can only admire their skill and understanding of the mathematics involved.

In the fifteenth century clock jacks were introduced. These mechanically operated figures were designed to strike the bell. Some old clock jacks are still at work and others have been replaced by replicas fashioned in fibreglass. One of the interesting things about clock jacks is the costume they wear. This usually gives us a clue to their age (or to the age of the originals if they are modern copies). Jack-smite-the-clock at St Edmunds, Southwold, Suffolk, shows us the manner in which a fifteenth-century Man-at-Arms was dressed. Shakespeare mentions clock jacks in Richard II ('I stand fooling here like Jack o' the Clock') and again in Richard III ('Like a Jack thou keepest thy stroke'). At Abinger Hammer, Surrey, a modern jack on the village hall holds a hammer and so provides us with a visual representation (a rebus) of the village's name.

78

The accuracy of clocks was improved when a pendulum clock was invented, in 1657, by the Dutch mathematician Christian Huygens. In the late seventeenth century a new design of escapement was invented – the anchor escapement. These two features were often combined. Another improvement made at this time was the introduction of a single hand. Clockfaces then showed four divisions between each hour. Examples of these one-handed veterans can be seen at Ightham Moat, Kent; Northill, Beds, and the splendid 16½ft dial at Coningsby, Lincs.

Victoria's Jubilees (1887 and 1897) provided a suitable excuse for the erection of clocks which often bear her initials and a date. At Baslow, Derbyshire, instead of the usual numerals round the clockface we can read 'Victoria 1897'. The 'O' is in the 12 position and the '8' at 6 o'clock. At West Acre, Norfolk, the inscription round the clockface reads 'Watch And Pray'. Buckland-in-the-Moor, Devon, provides us with another example 'My Dear Mother'.

If you have time on your hands clocks can become a consuming hobby. However, even casual observers can admire these mechanisms which were usually made to measure in days long before the concept of mass production had taken shape.

LEFT
Whixley, West Riding, Yorks: A dial with a message. Arthur Gaunt FRGS

RIGHT
Wooton Rivers, Wilts: This church clock was made by a village genius, Jack Spratt, to commemorate the coronation of King George V in 1911. Jack Spratt was born at Wooton Rivers in 1858. He apparently made his first clock when he was a boy to wake him for his daily work on a farm. The coronation clock was made from scrap items collected by the villagers and its parts include bicycle spindles and a sledge hammer to strike the bell. A broom handle serves as a pendulum. Its lead ⏤⏤⏤⏤⏤⏤ ⏤⏤⏤⏤⏤ ⏤⏤⏤⏤⏤ ⏤⏤⏤⏤⏤⏤⏤ put his timepiece together. The southern face bears the letters GLORY BE TO GOD. Clive Street

Memorials

The most vulnerable of churchyard memorials are the wooden graveboards which were favoured by those who could not afford the more durable kind. Sometimes you can just decipher the painted inscription. Graveboards usually seem to be placed in the less conspicuous parts of the churchyard.

East Bergholt, Suffolk: Most readers will be familiar with John Constable's famous painting of Willy Lott's cottage. William Lott lies buried near the south porch of the parish church and each year, although many visitors to the Constable country hurry to see his cottage, they miss his simple memorial. He died aged 88 on 12th July 1819.

Almost every country churchyard has its share of interesting or unusual names. The members of the Dark family recorded here did not gain a place in our history books, but we can see that William and Elizabeth shared a personal sorrow.

John Brown is a name we often associate with the American Civil War. His namesake, however, lived in Devon and 'was killed by a fall from a Cart' in 1831.

Urns, cherubs and scrolls are common elements in Georgian memorials. The situation of a memorial in a shady part of the churchyard may allow it to gather a crust of lichen.

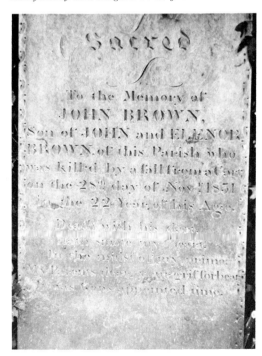

The nineteenth century saw various changes in the design of memorials and the lettering that masons employed. This example with its triple head – a symbol of the Trinity – includes an urn, stars and the sun's rays.

This eighteenth-century headstone in slate is distinguished by the lasting clarity of its simple lettering.

Eyam, Derbyshire: In 1665 the Plague was carried to Eyam in a box of clothing. The rector William Mompesson persuaded the villagers to stay put and thus prevented the infection spreading throughout the county. His wife was among the victims and this photograph shows her tomb which shelters beneath a spreading yew. Visitors should also see the Mompesson Well where the beleaguered villagers left money for the goods delivered to them from the outside world. Frank Rodgers.

Towers and Spires

Evercreech, Somerset: An essay in pinnacles which rise high above the village in typical perpendicular splendour. Above the aisles and clerestory there is a fine collection of gargoyles. A statue of St Peter gazes down from the tower and overlooks the modern street.

Bladon, Oxon: A church made famous since Sir Winston Churchill was laid to rest within its shade. Between the crocketed pinnacles there is a typical weathercock.

Hagworthingham, Lincs: A wide squat tower which shows various signs of rebuilding. Portions of it may be as old as the Saxon era, but the upper stage of the tower with its lancet windows is in the fashion of the thirteenth century. Note the heavy grave slabs in the foreground.

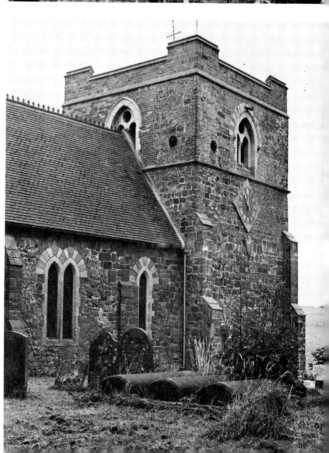

Haddiscoe, Norfolk: Round towers are quite numerous in East Anglia and some of them are amazingly old. That a flint tower's rubble walls should last some thousand years may surprise us. The shape itself, however, provides us with the reason. There are no corners to wear away and allow the structure to collapse. Below the corbels we can see the tri-angular-headed Saxon windows. Above them the chequered battlements provide us with an example of later workmanship.
Jeffery Whitelaw

Surfleet, Lincs: This tower with its definite inclination to avoid the vertical shows us that distant Pisa does not have a monopoly. The village is situated on the bank of the River Glen in the Lincolnshire fenland. As you approach the village along the A16 the six-foot lean of the spire catches the eye.

ABOVE
Eaton, Leics: A typical tower of Norman origin with a spire and pinnacles from a later age. Many churches are set on hill-tops like this one – which overlooks the Vale of Belvoir. Hill-tops were often used as places of Pagan worship and when Christianity replaced the old ideas churches were sometimes erected on these ancient sacred sites.

BELOW
Soulbury, Bucks: This view of another hilltop church allows us to see how so many of them slowly developed. The tower is at the western end and the nave (centre) has been enlarged by the addition of an aisle which has a porch to protect the south door. At the eastern end the chancel has a high-pitched tiled roof. A look at the windows tells us that they originated at various times from the thirteenth to the fifteenth century.

85

ABOVE
Thaxted, Essex: One of East Anglia's most graceful spires rising from walls of flint and stone. Not all churches have such interesting exteriors but the rich ornament we can see here is partly due to Thaxted's former importance for wool and cutlery. The base of the spire is supported by flying buttresses which spring from the decorated pinnacles.

ABOVE RIGHT
Crowland, Lincs: St Guthlac founded a monastery here in the seventh century. By the Middle Ages it had become one of the most important religious houses in the land. When the humble Guthlac made his way here, Crowland (often written Croyland in the past) was no more than an island in the watery fens. The present church was the north aisle of the monastic church which

was gradually dismantled after the Dissolution. To the right of the tower the west wall of the old nave gives us an impression of the Abbey's former architectural magnificence. The rows of statues include Guthlac, former abbots and other benefactors. The porch and inconsequential spire date from the sixteenth century.

BELOW LEFT
A conversation piece. Two bishops ruminate on the Abbey's decline.

BELOW
Earls Barton, Northants: The Saxon tower which has been standing for a thousand years.

Gargoyles

The name gargoyle is borrowed from the Old French 'gargouille' – meaning a throat. These peculiar faces do have a serious purpose. Where the edge of a roof is hidden by a parapet the rainwater has to be given an outlet. Gargoyles came into fashion in the fourteenth century and were the masons' answer to a very practical problem. Men in those times had strange ideas about devils and the fabulous creatures which inhabited the underworld. Monsters as well as men and angels appear in the gallery of gargoyles, which can be found on many of our parish churches. The quality of the stone used in different areas is not uniform. Harder stones wear well but many of the limestones are soft and show considerable signs of erosion. Weathering can make a grotesque gargoyle even more peculiar than the mason intended.

Objects created by a craftsman usually share a common style which cannot be mistaken. The manner in which ears or eyes are formed may provide us with an indication that they are the work of the same hand. If you study all the gargoyles on a building you may be able to decide if they are the work of one man or of several.

Very often there are a number of faces to be seen decorating the top of a church wall. These are sometimes mistakenly called gargoyles. They are really corbel brackets which help to take the thrust of the roof. You cannot mistake a genuine gargoyle if you look at its mouth!

ABOVE
Perhaps the work of an apprentice. The mouth is off centre.

BELOW
Sometimes they hide behind modern plumbing.

ABOVE
A nesting place?

BELOW
This odd-man-out is really a corbel bracket.

87

Furniture

Breamore, Hants: A Saxon arch in the south wall of the nave, bearing an inscription in Runic letters, which probably dates from the reign of Ethelred II (979–1016).

Ashton, Devon: The Elizabethan pulpit with its canopy. On the right the iron hour glass stand can still be seen. To the left of the doorway leading to the rood loft steps, the original door hinges are still in situ. The rood screen has painted panels depicting various saints.

ABOVE LEFT
Horwood, Devon: An armorial bench-end of the fifteenth century. The two shields show a demi horse rising from the water and a chevron between three cocks.

ABOVE RIGHT
Horwood, Devon: Two saints or Apostles in fifteenth-century apparel.

RIGHT
Barking, Suffolk: This brazier, one of a pair, provided central heating for the congregation. The lid was removed to allow burning charcoal to be placed in the bowl. Clive Street

Royal Arms

From the time of Henry VIII the Royal Arms were to be
found exhibited in our parish churches. They were usually
placed at the east end of the nave. The congregation, therefore,
would enjoy a weekly reminder of the source of temporal
power. To a student of heraldry these tablets are full of fascination. This example bears a date (1682) and the initials of the
reigning monarch (Charles II). The shield of arms is
surrounded by the Garter motto and supported by a lion and a
unicorn. Above the shield there is the helm which is surmounted
by a crown bearing another lion. When Henry V fought at
Agincourt (1415) he bore a royal shield which included the
three fleurs-de-lis of France; a reminder of the English claim
to the French throne. On this Stuart shield we see the arms of
France (modern) quartered with the three leopards of England.
The rampant lion represents Scotland and the harp Ireland.

Repton, Derbyshire: This Saxon crypt has rudimentary pillars which have cable moulding and crude cushion capitals. Frank Rodgers

Weston Turville, Bucks: A splendid roof which has much in common with many ancient barns and timbered houses. (See also page 21)

The Chapel

Nonconformity in England grew up in an age of social and political conflict. It is very easy to forget just how hard our ancestors had to struggle to win the freedom to worship in their own way. Almost every village seems to have a Nonconformist building of some sort. To distinguish between them and the established Church we often call the former 'chapels'.

In the remote days when nonconformity could bring violent persecution it took a good deal of courage to remain true to one's convictions. The Congregational Church has its origins in the late sixteenth century, but most of its existing buildings are not as old.

Baptist Chapels are also a familiar feature of the village scene. John Bunyan, who so inspired Baptist thought, suffered imprisonment among other indignities for his Faith. His home at Elstow, Bedfordshire, is now a place of pilgrimage. The Society of Friends (Quakers) probably suffered the most collective abuse in the early days. Its members refused to meet in secret. The Society was founded by George Fox in 1668. Nonconformists first met in private houses. The style and scale of nonconformist architecture often reflects its domestic origins. In earlier days the term Meeting House was frequently used for places of Nonconformist worship. There are several Meeting Houses of architectural interest: like those at Jordans, Bucks; Yealand Conyers and Briggflatts, Westmorland.

Nonconformists had to wait for a long time before political convenience provided them with the freedom to worship in their own way, without 'let or hindrance'. The statute which provided this freedom was the Toleration Act of 1689 (1 William and Mary cap 18). Under its provisions freedom of worship was assured. The arrangement which united all Protestants served the purposes of William III who, at that time, had one eye on the deposed, Roman Catholic, James II.

The design of 'Meeting Houses' built after 1689 followed the same influences which we have noted in the sphere of domestic buildings. During the eighteenth century and up to the Gothic Revival most Chapels were functional, simple and even plain in their appearance. Today this simplicity can often be refreshing.

One more Nonconformist Church which has an architectural tradition of its own is the Methodist Movement which was founded by John and Charles Wesley in the late eighteenth century. Perhaps it is significant that the Congregationalists, Baptists and even the established Church still use many of the hymns they wrote.

ABOVE
The architectural style of the typical Nonconformist chapel was usually as simple and unpretentious as the inscription to be found on its exterior.

BELOW
Withypool, Somerset: A Chapel with Gothic leanings. Notice the ogee moulding and the dripstones above the windows.

Cookham, Berks: An old Chapel with a new use. It now houses a collection of paintings and objects associated with the artist, Sir Stanley Spencer, who lived in the village.

Heptonstall, West Riding, Yorks: The oldest existing Methodist Chapel which was opened in 1764. Arthur Gaunt FRGS

The School

One or two village schools are ancient. A few originated in the seventeenth or eighteenth centuries. Most have their architectural origins in the Gothic Revival. The first parish schools it seems were conducted by the priest, if he was interested enough, in a corner of the church. Eventually a room in a cottage became more suitable and by slow degrees the idea of providing a purpose-built schoolhouse gained approval. The schools which were used in the years following the Civil War often contained living quarters for a resident master. In those days all schoolmasters were supposed to be licensed by the bishop before they could practise. The limitations imposed on Dissenters meant that the established Church had a tight hold on these early schools. In the early years of the eighteenth century the Society for Promoting Christian Knowledge (SPCK) sponsored the development of hundreds of village schools. Originally these were promoted with the joint support of Anglicans and Nonconformists. The partnership did not last, however, but once the schools had been established many seem to have survived well into the next century.

Frequent references to 'Dame Schools' will be found in local records. These Dame Schools appear to have flourished in the eighteenth century, but they should not be confused with the Charity Schools set up by bequests or the subscriptions raised by the SPCK and its supporters. Dame Schools probably served a practical purpose imposed by the economic problems besetting the rural poor. If mother could go to work unencumbered by small children her potential earnings were greater. The pence spent at the Dame's child-minding establishment made higher earnings possible. Most Dame Schools probably waxed and waned with seasonal demand. They kept no formal records. No doubt there were Dame Schools where instruction of a good standard was provided. Most merely kept the children in a safe place while mother added to the family income.

A nineteenth-century school constructed in stone and slate. Above the schoolroom there is a clock and a bell cote. The teacher's house completes the composition and follows the same Gothic style beloved by Victorian philanthropy. It is a long time since scholars made their daily pilgrimage to the school door. Since the schoolroom has become part of the dwelling the dormers on each side of the bell-gable have been added.

Charity Schools were sometimes erected but no funds were provided for the schoolmaster's stipend. When this situation arose a school could stand unused for long periods. It is usually possible to identify a school but some look just like houses and can easily be missed.

The rivalry between Anglicans and Nonconformists reared its head once more in the nineteenth century. A British and Foreign Schools Society and the National Society were established to promote schools in every parish in the land. We can still see the names British School and National School carved above the portals of some of these buildings. Numerically speaking there seem to be many more National (Church of England) Schools.

After the 1870 Education Act another kind of school came into being. Where voluntary effort had failed to provide a school, a self-governing School Board was set up. The School Boards were responsible for the construction of buildings, but sometimes a Board took over an existing voluntary school. Board Schools are usually associated with urban society. Hundreds of Board Schools however, were, erected in the countryside. As far as architecture is concerned the Board School's image is more or less inseparable from the Neo-Gothic tradition. The Board School system lasted until 1901 when another Education Act created the County Education Committees (the LEAs) which exist today. The Local Education Authorities took over the autonomous functions of the separate Boards and for the first time there was a co-ordinated local system of elementary education. After 1901 a few 'Council' schools were also built in rural surrounds. Things have changed in the countryside since the first charity schools were established in Cromwell's England. Some villages have lost their schools altogether and even young children travel away from home for their education. Redundant schools are usually converted into dwellings and still remain part of the village scene.

Not all Victorian schools were built in the fashionable style. This example has an attractive gable which owes much to Dutch influence. Although the school is situated in quite a small village there were separate entrances for boys and girls.

Bells called the faithful to worship and the scholar to his tasks. This bell was cast in the seventeenth century and bears the name of the schoolmaster.

The old Grammar School at Dorchester Abbey, Oxon.

A Charity School (c1724).
Soulbury, Bucks.

Chaddesley-Corbett, Worcs: A mixture of ideas and materials.
The arches show Gothic leanings, but the gables remind us that
this is a part of England where the timber tradition is strong.

The Almshouse

In the Middle Ages the aged and infirm were cared for in the hospitals – 'spitals' – which followed a monastic style of organisation. The ideas and principles such institutions upheld were no doubt influenced by the Order of the Knights Hospitallers which had been involved in the Crusades. A hospital had an obligation to provide refreshment for travellers and to this day the weary may claim the Wayfarer's Dole at the gate of the Hospital of St Cross, a mile or so outside Winchester's City Walls. Many of the hospitals suffered the same fate as the monasteries in 1547. The need for charity did not disappear, however, and from Elizabeth I's time onwards a new style of provision was made for the elderly poor.

Almshouses were usually erected at the expense of a single beneficiary. Most seem to derive from bequests and it is common for the fabric to bear a visible and clear indication of its creator's identity. The architectural shape seldom deviates from the terrace idea, but the style depends upon the time of origin. It is possible to find almshouses which also incorporate a schoolhouse, but this arrangement is not common. Sometimes a bequest set out rigid requirements for admission in addition to an assumed poverty. There was no room for Dissenters! Residence sometimes demanded the wearing of a common dress. In the changed society of today the almshouses are still well used. Some enjoy an income which derives from additional bequests.

As far as the external features are concerned you will not find any two groups of almshouses which look exactly alike. They were designed to serve the needs of a particular village, and village worthies or the donor's survivors decided the architectural details. Sometimes very original buildings – like the one at Stydd – were the result of their deliberations. Most conform to an accepted domestic tradition which we have noted at the beginning of this book. All, however, have points of interest which can give us an insight into the way our ancestors considered their less-fortunate fellows and the chance to perpetuate their family name. The village almshouse has a comfortable mellow look to twentieth-century eyes. It has served the needs of the village so well and it would be sad indeed if such institutions perished.

At the beginning of the nineteenth century a Parliamentary investigation was made into all parish charities. The Reports of the Commissioners were printed – in large volumes. The local reference library should be able to provide a copy for your county. The reports usually give a considerable amount of detailed information about the establishment of a charity and its original requirements, eg 'That none should wander abroad to beg, nor keep any tippling within the said house, or should use unlawful games, or be a frequenter of alehouses . . .' and 'Every of them to have yearly a gown on All Saints' Day of the price or value of 13s 4d, and upon the left sleeve of every of the said gowns, there should be set a red cross. . . .' Like so many other things in the village the almshouse had a style of its own.

Ellesborough, Bucks: An inscription setting out the origin of the almshouses. This one provides details of the charity's terms of reference – which was one way of making sure they were not forgotten. Notice the use of Roman numerals.

Quainton, Bucks: This elegant tablet with its cartouche showing the Winwood arms provides us with an interesting example of seventeenth-century lettering. Above the coronet with its bird there is a blocked window opening which has been painted in casement fashion.

Thaxted, Essex: Disused almshouses with low-pitched dormer windows. Almshouses were probably the first terraced dwellings built in the countryside. These follow a simple rustic fashion

with plain doors and diamond-paned windows. The bedroom windows must be almost at floor level.

Stydd, Lancs: An almshouse to be inhabited by six ladies was established here under the will of John Shireburn (obit 1726). W. Fairclough contributed a sketch of it in 1948 to Recording Britain Vol. III (Oxford University Press). *Most almshouses follow a conventional pattern and their features usually reflect local traditions. This example is a fascinating and unexplained architectural curiosity. There is an almost Mediterranean look in its steps and balcony.* Tom Parker

The Workhouse

The attitude to poverty began to change in the early nineteenth century. Enclosure of common land, and the loss of the means to eke out a subsistence diet from the soil, created legions of rural poor. Even an expanding industrial demand for manpower could not redress the balance. The problem was too vast for the traditional almshouse to solve. Almshouses alone were too small and too few. In an effort to combat poverty the Poor Law Amendment Act (1834) provided for inter-parish co-operation. Hitherto each parish had to fend for itself. The new order presented the prospect of united parishes (Unions) with a common workhouse. Some of these 'Unions' were constructed on the fringe of country towns but larger villages attracted their share.

From the architectural point of view the workhouse followed classical lines, without any unnecessary decoration. In plan the building usually has two or more wings which are arranged to create a courtyard. A portico often appears at the main entrance, but within public charity was as cold and hard as iron. The cosy concept of the almshouse with man and wife sharing the same dwelling did not matter here. Segregation by age, sex and infirmity was an obvious public economy to make. Sentiment had no place in the Union's draughty and dismal corridors. People did not come here; only 'paupers' came to work or die. These gaunt monuments enshrine society's disregard for its detritus. They will always look gaunt and cold to those who know what sadness soaked into their walls. Once within the building a man, woman or child was a mere cipher in the Superintendent's book. Small wonder so many preferred to jump into the oblivion of a rushing weir. The term pauper remained in official use until the social reforms of c1908. Like the workhouse it was a long time dying.

5
Pride
and Prejudice

The village street, like most others, is now dominated by the motor car. These days, to cross in safety we must have our wits about us and dare not dally in the roadway. Our grandfathers had less to fear and for them it was a commonplace matter to hold counsel with their fellows anywhere on the highway. Children used the road too – as a playground – and had little to fear from the sedate pace of the sparse horse-drawn traffic. For hundreds of years villagers enjoyed the freedom of the village street. The motor age has filched this freedom from us. It is to be hoped that the time may come when the wheeled menace will be expelled from parts of our villages and country dwellers too can enjoy the benefits of those pedestrian-only areas which town planners have so recently 'invented'.

Some of the oldest survivals to be found along the highway are the ancient crosses which long ago provided a pulpit for travelling preachers. A few crosses may be older than the parish church itself. Eventually the open cross was provided with a roof. The subject of preaching crosses is enough to fill a book and space will allow but one to be shown here.

Preachers and pedlars had a common interest in attracting as large a crowd as possible. The situation of a village cross made it just as useful to those with a commercial instead of a

spiritual turn of mind. For this reason the village cross often became a place of business and eventually the cross had to share its place or give way to a market house. Some market houses seem to have grown round a cross, but they all display an individuality which is unique.

One of the responsibilities of each parish, in the days before there was a police force, was to appoint a constable each year to uphold the Queen's peace. This office is at least as ancient as the thirteenth century. Our language has provided several names for this important parish officer who was also titled headborough, thirdborough, borsholder or tithing man. His symbol of office was the constable's staff and most local museums have a selection on display. It was the constable's duty to arrest any offender and keep him, or her, in a place of safety until a magistrate was able to consider the facts. Many parishes provided a substantial lock-up or cage for those awaiting trial. These structures always display a typical rugged style of their own which cannot be mistaken. The unwilling inmates perhaps found that justice too had an equally rugged countenance.

Thaxted, Essex: One of the things which distinguished a village's importance was the possession of a civic building. This splendid market house rises in three impressive stages above the village street. Below the open arches village elders can still sit and discuss the affairs of the day. Above their heads the visitor can still see a firehook which was an essential tool to have at hand in the days when most houses were thatched.

Law and Order

LEFT

Thaxted, Essex: An alternative to the stocks was the village lock-up – or clink. Such premises no doubt needed a strong door with a sound lock. The ventilation of the village cage was usually rudimentary.

BELOW

Long Crendon, Bucks: The building known as the Court-house. It is now a National Trust property and the upper floor which once served as a wool store is open to the public. This jettied timber house is particularly interesting as its end bay (right) follows the Wealden style – with its recessed wall and diagonal braces. (See also page 19)

RIGHT

Walsingham, Norfolk: A multi-purpose building which serves as a cage, beacon and a conduit – notice the protruding cast-iron spout on the right. This ancient structure has been repaired and some of the original stonework around the door has been replaced with brick. Clive Street

Breedon, Leics: The conical roof of this village lock-up is surmounted by a handsome weathercock. Like so many doors this one has a robust appearance and heavy studs. There is a very small panel in the door to admit light. Arthur Gaunt FRGS

Norton, Shropshire: These dual-purpose stocks retain their handcuffs at the top of the whipping post.

Wainfleet All Saints, Lincs: Although the modern guidebooks call Wainfleet a town its population in 1801 was 506 souls. This ancient cross still stands in the wide square which is surrounded by houses of brick and pantiles. The windvane at the top is unusual and not as old as the stonework. This style of cross is known as the shaft-on-steps type. It looks rather like an old-fashioned candlestick. Wainfleet is situated, appropriately enough, in the old wapentake of Candleshoe.

Wheatley, Oxon: A pyramid of parochial power.

6
The Inn

The origin of the inn seems to be derived from the hospitality once provided by the monasteries to travel weary pilgrims. In places where the number of pilgrims exceeded the accommodation available extra houses were erected for them. The 'George' at Glastonbury, Somerset, originated in this way. Towns probably had inns before they appeared in villages and as long ago as Chaucer's time pilgrims lodged at the 'Tabard' in Southwark. When Englishmen began to travel around the shires in coaches the demand for inns increased. Eventually the stage coach added to the number and needs of those abroad on the highways at nightfall. Inns had to provide lodging for the traveller and stables for the horses. You cannot mistake an inn which dates from coaching days. Apart from an obvious archway wide enough for a coach to pass, within the inn yard, there is an array of stables and lofts where fodder was stored.

Inn signs guided the traveller to the place where he could find food and shelter. The use of trade signs goes back as far as Pompeii and they were to be found in abundance in the streets of medieval England. Many signs have a religious significance like the Lamb and Flag which is the emblem of Our Lord – see St John's Gospel 1:29. The catalogue of inn signs is almost inexhaustible. As far as village inns are concerned they do not always display signs exclusively associated with the countryside. There are frequent borrowings from heraldry and some signs assert loyalty to the Monarch. Ploughs, bulls, harrows, wheatsheaves and the various tools employed by village craftsmen naturally abound. The recent revival of pictorial signs is to be applauded as they represent a tradition and style of their own.

BELOW
Chilterns: A living sign in yew which is taller than 'The Yew Tree' itself.

BELOW
Hants/Sussex border: The inn was often a place of rest for tired drovers who walked their flocks to market.

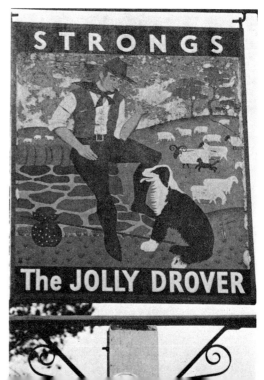

ABOVE LEFT
A Warwickshire inn sign showing an old-style cider mill. This primitive device was used to squeeze out the juice from the (crab) apples.

ABOVE RIGHT
Wrantage, Somerset: The gable of this inn has been decorated with a number of farming bygones. Part of a harrow, hames, a ball and chain for a gate and a side-handled hay knife can be seen.

RIGHT
Old Weston, Hunts: The 'Black Swan'.

107

ABOVE

Combe Martin, Devon: One of England's most curious inns was designed to resemble a pack of cards.

BELOW

Long Marston, Herts: English monarchs have provided names for many country inns which no doubt adopted them in the best patriotic spirit. Queen Elizabeth I has been a popular subject and gave the signpainter a splendid opportunity to show his skill.

RIGHT
Withypool, Somerset: A name which recalls the events which led a monarch to seek refuge in an oak tree.

BELOW LEFT
Putney Heath, Surrey: This sign seems to portray a highwayman but Tibbet was, in fact, a gamekeeper. He carried a pistol to protect himself in case he met up with armed poachers.
Arthur Gaunt FRGS

BELOW
Cragg Vale, Yorks: A portrait of England's folk-hero Robin Hood who had the habit of leaving by the back door when the Sheriff came in the front. Arthur Gaunt FRGS

ABOVE LEFT
Another creature from the greenwoods.

ABOVE
Gotham, Notts: This sign is a reminder of the legendary men of the village who feigned madness to dissuade King John from building a hunting lodge. One of their escapades involved making a fence round a cuckoo to enable them to enjoy its song all the year round. Frank Rodgers

LEFT
Chilterns: Birds are also favourite subjects for inn signs. This device was sure to attract custom from the gamekeeper.

RIGHT
Buckinghamshire: This sign is based on a design to be found in the Washburn Valley, Yorks, and in some other places. It has a rarity value nevertheless.

BELOW LEFT
Berwick St James, Wilts: At first there is no obvious reason for a boot to be found on an inn sign. This military version is far removed from the legend which inspired so many 'Boot Inns'. In the Middle Ages a priest – John Schorne – at North Marston, Bucks, was credited with conjuring the Devil into a boot. The village became a place of pilgrimage after his death and his body was eventually removed to Windsor. Representations of John Schorne holding the boot with the Devil's head peeping out of the top can be found on the chancel screens of several churches. There are examples in East Anglia and Devon (Alphington) which show how wide-spread this popular tale used to be. The story may also have been the origin of the Jack-in-the-Box.

BELOW RIGHT
Derbyshire: A sign in a cartouche with an heraldic crest for good measure. The blacksmith was able to add his skill to the woodcarver's in the making of this attractive signboard and its bracket. Frank Rodgers

THIS GATE HANGS HIGH
AND HINDERS NONE
SOME CIDER TAKE
AND TRAVEL ON

GATE | CIDER HOUSE

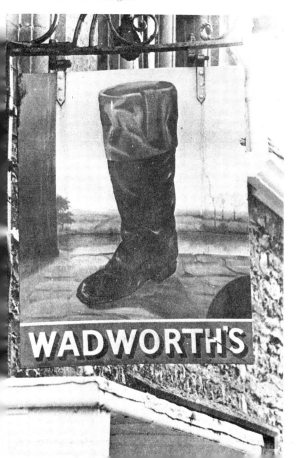

WADWORTH'S

THE JUG AND GLASS

The Smiths Arms - The smallest Public House in England, originally a blacksmith's shop.
King Charles II stopped here to have his horse shod, he asked for a drink & the
blacksmith replied 'I have no license Sire', so, there & then the King granted him one

CHE SARA SARA

A · B · C

ABOVE
*Godmanstone, Dorset: The sign above what is said to be the
smallest inn in England. It illustrates one of the privileges
folklore ascribed to the smith – the right to hang horseshoes
upside down without the 'luck' falling out.* Frank Rodgers

LEFT
*A sign showing the arms of the lord of the manor who no doubt
once owned the whole village.*

RIGHT
*A horse, cobbles and cross-keys. The latter is a sign attributed
to St Peter.*

ABOVE
The constellation Ursa Major – the plough – often provides inspiration for the sign painter. This design contains the other more earthy kind of plough as well.

BELOW
The eighteenth-century's contribution to our transport system is conveyed in an attractive way by Stanley Chew in this elegant board.

ABOVE
A black horse was an obvious alternative to a white one. There is a lot of fascinating history attached to such designs which provided the basis for The Black Horsemen *by S. G. Wildman – a book all sign enthusiasts should not fail to read.*

BELOW
Cookham, Berks: An old-style ferry operated by a winch with passengers suitably attired.

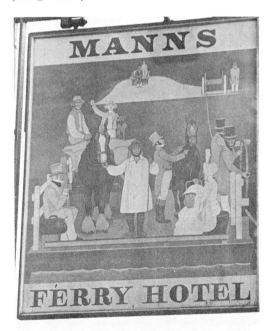

7
Windmills

Windmills have been a feature of the English scene since the thirteenth century or thereabouts. The genius who contrived this curious machine remains anonymous, but whoever it was we can attribute to him an original turn of mind. There is an often-repeated tradition which assigns the introduction of the windmill into England to the period of the Crusaders. This may quite possibly be true, but the Middle East seems to abound in mills with masonry towers and not the timber windmill which was certainly constructed here in the medieval period. Perhaps it would be nearer the truth to suggest that mills seen by travellers during pilgrimage inspired ideas which were translated into timber traditions on reaching home. It is probably significant to note the reliance our early millwrights placed on wood rather than masonry. In regions where winds are more constantly in a given quarter the construction of a mill with a fixed aspect was practicable. Such circumstances do not apply in our colder northern latitudes and for a windmill to be used effectively in the British Isles it had to be capable of facing its sails towards any degree of the compass.

The mill from Danzey Green, near Tamworth-in-Arden, Warwicks, which is shown here under reconstruction at the Avoncroft Museum of Buildings, Stoke Prior, Bromsgrove. The body of this mill is supported by a main post and a series of wheels running on a curb at the top of the round house wall. Mills with this feature are sometimes called composite mills. There is another example to be seen at Madingley, Cambs. Among the other buildings to be seen at Avoncroft is an Iron Age dwelling, a chainmaker's workshop, a nailmaker's workshop, a granary, a fifteenth-century merchant's house, and an old inn. This is an important museum which has ambitious plans to preserve much more of our architectural heritage.

Our knowledge of the early English windmills comes from several sources. Medieval manuscripts which were so skilfully and delightfully illustrated by observant artists and calligraphers provide us with some of the most detailed and reliable information. Other sources include the various decorations found in church windows as at Fairford, Glos; or carved in wood, eg at Bishop's Lydeard, Somerset. Mapmakers too have left us a legacy of information on the estate and village maps drawn usually for the benefit of feudal lords. Windmills by their very nature make good landmarks. While the quality of surveyors' draughtsmanship often varies, and is sometimes very elementary, enough evidence survives to persuade us that the early mills followed a common structural pattern.

It may be misleading to assume that the early windmill was the product of an English mind in isolation. Identical mills exist in Holland and by the thirteenth century there was a regular commercial link between England and Europe which must also have had technological implications. The strong probability that some design elements incorporated in English mills were derived from Europe must not be ignored. Another con-

sideration which cannot be overlooked arises from the fact that Dutch mills have a history which can be traced from the same period of time (see *The Dutch Windmill* by Frederick Stokhuyzen, 1963, English Edition, Universe Books Inc., New York).

All our early mills shared the same characteristics. They had a small body, mounted on a vertical post, which could be turned in any desired direction so that the mill sails could face into the wind. The sails were simple wooden frames upon which the canvas was rigged. Windmills have a close affinity to ships. When the wind was strong a minimum of sail was required and when the wind was light all the sails had to be fully rigged. There was one disadvantage to this primitive arrangement. If the wind's force changed the mill had to be stopped to enable the miller to adjust the canvas.

ABOVE LEFT

The obliging miller at Bocking (Essex) made good use of the roundhouse wall to advertise his services to passers-by. We can note the ominous addition of steam power which eventually was responsible for putting many mills out of business. The last working days of many windmillers were spent grinding grist (for livestock) in place of the flour which had been their pride in former years. Bocking Mill has been restored and is open to visitors who will find that the roundhouse now shelters a fascinating collection of milling relics.

RIGHT

Great Bardfield, Essex: This splendid mill is known as Gibraltar Mill, but the name has been in use so long that no one can say why it was bestowed. At its base it is octagonal. The top of the tower (c1750) is circular and on it sits one of the sleekest boat-shaped caps – which looks just like an up-turned dinghy. Since 1904 the mill has had a fantail. In later years a single-storey dwelling has been added to the tower. Just inside the gateway an iron gear wheel can be seen decorating the garden steps. Although this outstanding mill is a private dwelling a thoughtful owner has installed floodlights so that its features may enhance even the night skies.

LEFT

Heckington, Lincs: This mill is a unique survivor of the seven English eight-sailed mills. The tower was built in the early part of the nineteenth century, but the cap came from a Boston mill in 1892. In its working days the sails powered five pairs of stones and a saw mill. To prevent storm damage the shutters were left out when the sails were restored in the 1950s. The mill is owned by the Kesteven County Council. Visitors can inspect the interior and the key is available at all reasonable times from the miller's cottage.

8
Going
Places

Travelling on wheels it seems has always been a costly business. The piecemeal attention our road system was given by individual parishes in the Middle Ages was ineffective to say the least. Most historians agree that the eighteenth century marked a turning point in our society. One of its important developments was the demand for more and better roads. Individual Acts of Parliament created the Turnpike Trusts which maintained and improved given roadways. Each Trust had its scale of tolls and set up milestones and toll houses for the collection of its revenue. English individuality once again asserted itself and our surviving toll houses reflect the wide architectural preferences of different Trustees. Classical and Gothic fashions were followed and the resulting variety still adds charm and interest to our roadsides.

The law required Turnpike Trusts to erect milestones. This enabled users to see how far they had travelled and provided some check on the tolls levied by the toll keeper. The turnpike system proper did in fact, last until the 1880s but some tolls – like Swinford, Oxon – are still in operation. Eighteenth-century mileposts were fashioned in stone and followed the pattern set by the Romans. Mileposts set up in the 1800s were often made in cast iron, but they usually followed the patterns of their stone predecessors. Iron posts may bear the name of the ironfounder – look at the back at about ground level. The advanced speeds of the motor age make the relatively small lettering on the milepost difficult to read. As a result we have gradually come to accept larger and larger signs. Those currently erected (in the name of progress?)

disfigure, distract and destroy the scale of visual values. They are utterly at odds with our roadside tradition.

There was a time, in 1939, when the humble milestone – along with the signposts – was held to have a strategic significance. To confuse an invader, who could presumably not read a map, all signs were removed and stored away until better days. When they were replaced some roadmen had understandably forgotten exactly where they came from. One-inch Ordnance Survey maps of the 1930s will show you where the mileposts should be. Those who search them out may find them even a furlong or two away from their time-honoured locations. Mileposts can become casualties of road 'improvements' and vigilance is often necessary to make sure that they do not suddenly become so much hardcore. One of the interesting things about mileposts is the varied styles of lettering they display.

Signposts may be as old as mileposts. Their pointing fingers gained them the name 'handing' or 'finger' posts. England's oldest example is probably the one at Broadway,

Worcs, which was set up by Nathaniel Izod
in 1669. Such things were in those days left to
personal initiative. In common with the milepost, local preference for particular details of
design, make their features a rewarding study.

For those who are not in a hurry to reach
their destination before the motorist in front,
the roadside holds many treasures.

Milestones

ABOVE LEFT
*Wiltshire: A good many milestones record the distance to
London. This one has an unusual curved head.*

LEFT
*Rousdon, Devon: A modern pillar which incorporates some
Gothic ideas. The reverse of the stone shows that it is also the
village War Memorial – a fact which may make it unique. Its
lettering is in a modern style and although it may not be large
enough for a speeding motorist, there can be no doubt that it
suits the subject to perfection.*

RIGHT
*Another interesting cast-iron post bearing a fraction. Leighton
is an established contraction for Leighton Buzzard (Beds).
Notice the distinctive size of the figures.*

Toll-Houses

Lincolnshire: A Gothic essay in pantiles and brick. The shape of the original doorway can still be seen between the two windows of the protruding bay. From the toll-keeper's point of view there were very practical reasons for having windows arranged so that he commanded a view in both directions.

A toll-house with an upper floor. Mathematical considerations seem to have determined the size of the dormer window. Windows and doors follow the ogee shape favoured in the fourteenth century. A vertical joint line in the brickwork suggests that the lean-to (right) was a later addition.

Signposts

Essex: An example of a typical finger-post with lettering which probably dates from the 1930s. Two of the places shown are on the banks of the River Colne. Both show how foreign elements abound in English place names. Engaine is derived from an Old French word meaning 'ingenuity'. White Colne comes from an error in translation. At the time of Domesday (1086) the manor was held by Dimidius Blancus. Bures, which has a homely sound, comes from an Old English word meaning cottage. Pebmarsh indicates pasture land. Alphamstone simply means the town or village of Aelfhelm.

Devon: It is refreshing to see that the dead hand of standardisation has not yet crept into the Devon byways. The practice of renewing old posts in the original style is to be applauded. To add the name of the post's location helps to assert its individuality. Three of the names shown here remind us of those well-known rivers Taw and Torridge. Harepie is a name which speaks for itself.

Letters carved into the wood in the fashion known to our ancestors. An example of a clear sign well executed and in accord with its surroundings.

ABOVE
West Wycombe, Bucks: A signpost set up on a pedestal in MDCCLII (1752).

BELOW
In 1951 the Bedfordshire County Council decided to celebrate the Festival of Britain by providing each village with new signs. Each sign also bore a representation of the County's arms and the Festival symbol.

ABOVE LEFT
The County arms with the lion and the bull supporting the shield.

ABOVE
An addition to the Bromham sign which shows that the villagers won the County's Best Kept Village Award in 1967.

ABOVE RIGHT
In another century this Festival symbol will become an antique like the mileposts shown above.

LEFT
Not all modern signs are objectionable. This Dartmoor Pony symbol, which welcomes visitors to one of our National Parks, shows what a little thought can achieve.

RIGHT
Snettisham, Norfolk: This village sign was presented by the local Women's Institute. It shows a gold torque of prehistoric origin – one was discovered in recent years – which is supported by two sea horses. A smugglers' boat and two smugglers – one with a lantern the other with a pistol – completes the design. Snettisham lies close to the Wash and in former years many a smuggler crossed the parish during darkness. Clive Street

9
Curiosities

With the passing of time objects which once had a perfectly respectable purpose became redundant. Such was the Englishman's former reluctance to dismember the artefacts of his ancestors' making that they usually survived. Some were attached to walls but others remained in the prominent positions they enjoyed during the days of their usefulness. The inventiveness of the countryman, and gentleman, did not always result in the creation of things specifically functional. Certain things were made for their looks alone and little importance was placed on their practical use. Topiary allowed the countryman to display his ability to shape nature into any likeness of his fancy. Gentlemen could indulge the same whims which were often expressed in the bricks and mortar of their often splendid, but usually useless follies. Among fanciful things we can number those tall memorial pillars and obelisks which dominate so many skylines around our shires. Such things were often erected to speak the praises of famous men but worthy people with local origins and importance were also commemorated in this way. It can take a long time for memorials to take shape. The venerable Maud Heath – see page 36 – had to wait a long while for the trustees of her charity to provide a public acknowledgement of her thoughtfulness. Even more years elapsed before a nineteenth-century vicar inspired the erection of her effigy – on the hillside overlooking the other end of her 'Causeway'.

It would not be difficult to fill a book with the quaint and curious survivals which are scattered throughout the length and breadth of England. The fragment of space which can be given to them here will provide no more than a starting point for those who wish to explore for themselves. There are curiosities which defy classification, others which declare their presence from miles away and some which lurk in their shyness among less-trodden paths. However they all share an enigmatic quality which makes the traveller stop and wonder.

The art of topiary was known to the Romans and no doubt during their stay in these islands the first British examples appeared only to be forgotten after the retreat of the Legions. It seems likely that the fashion for clipping hedges followed William I from Normandy in 1066. By the time of the Tudor monarchs it was to be seen in the knot garden which also provided the housemaids with somewhere to spread out their washing. The fashion eventually worked its way down from the great houses to influence the owners of cottage gardens. This interesting example is uncomplicated but pleasing to the eye.

Ammonite: These fascinating coiled fossils which vary in size from a fraction of an inch to perhaps as much as two feet can be found in many parts of Britain. The best known locations for present-day collectors are along the shore at Whitby (Yorks) and Charmouth – Lyme Regis (Dorset). Mary Anning (obit 1847) made this latter coastline famous when she discovered an ichthyosaurus there in 1811. The name of the ammonite, however, is derived from the fact that their shape was a reminder of the horns on the ram-god, known as Ammon by the Egyptians and Zeus Ammonis by the Greeks. The original creatures were shellfish which lived in the seas of the cainozoic and mesozoic eras – up to 180 million years ago. From the eighteenth century onwards larger specimens were frequently used as decorations on buildings or garden walls.

An evergreen stag.

Crowland, Lincs: A bridge which has three pointed arches each joining at the centre. This curious structure is really three half-bridges linked together. Once it allowed villagers to avoid the waters running beneath but the stream has now gone leaving the bridge high and dry. From the shape of the ribbed arches we can see that the builders lived in the thirteenth century.

ABOVE
Harpsden, Oxon: The gable of a barn decorated with eighteenth-century wall paper printing blocks.

BELOW
A detail of an intricate pattern.

LEFT
Three Shire Stone where Northamptonshire, Bedfordshire and Huntingdon meet on the A45.

Bibliography

No single book can hope to say everything about the English village. Even a bibliography will have its limitations but the works listed here will enable the reader to explore some of the many facets of the village scene which have been outlined above.

ARNOLD, JAMES, *The Shell Book of Country Crafts*. John Baker.

BARLEY, M. W., *The English Farmhouse and Cottage*. Routledge & Kegan Paul.

BETJEMAN, JOHN & PIPER, JOHN (Ed), *Shell Guides – to Cornwall, Dorset, Isle of Wight, Lincolnshire, Norfolk, Rutland, South-West Wales, Suffolk, Worcestershire, Essex, Gloucestershire, Kent, Leicestershire, Northumberland, Wiltshire, Northamptonshire*. Faber & Faber.

BEESON, C. F., *English Church Clocks 1280–1850*. Phillimore.

BEVAN-EVANS, M & JONES, W. HUGH, *Farmhouses and Cottages – An Introduction to Vernacular Architecture in Flintshire*. Flintshire Record Office, Hawarden.

BRAUN, HUGH, *Old English Houses*. Faber.

CLIFTON-TAYLOR, ALEC, *The Pattern of English Building*. Faber & Faber.

COOKE, A. O., *A Book of Dovecotes*. T. N. Foulis.

DAINTON, COURTNEY, *Clock Jacks and Bee Boles*. Phoenix.

DUNNICH, FREDA, *Cotswold Stone. Country Craftsmen*. Chapman and Hall.

EVANS, GEORGE EWART, *The Farm and the Village. Where Beards Wag All*. Faber.

GAUNT, ARTHUR, *Its Odd, Its Yorkshire, Tourists' England*. Frank Graham.

GRIGSON, GEOFFREY, *The Shell Country Alphabet*. Michael Joseph & George Rainbird.

HADFIELD, MILES (Ed), *A Book of Country Houses*. Country Life.

HAINES, GEORGE H., *Discovering Crosses*. Shire Publications.

HOGG, GARRY, *Odd Aspects of England*. David & Charles.

HOGG, WARRINGTON, *A Book of Sundials*. T. N. Foulis.

HOLLISTER-SHORT, G. J., *Discovering Wrought Iron*. Shire Publications.

HOWKINS, CHRISTOPHER, *Discovering Church Furniture*. Shire Publications.

JAMIESON, MICHAEL, *Coaching in the North Country*. Frank Graham.

JOBSON, ALLAN, *Household and Country Crafts*. Elek.

JONES, SYDNEY R., *English Village Homes*. Batsford.

KENWOOD, JAMES, *The Roof Tree*. Oxford.

LAMB, CADBURY & WRIGHT, GORDON, *Discovering Inn Signs*. Shire Publications.

LINDLEY, KENNETH, *Of Graves and Epitaphs*. Hutchinson. *Graves and Graveyards*. Routledge & Kegan Paul.

LOFTHOUSE, JESSICA, *Portrait of Lancashire. Countrygoer's North*. Robert Hale.

MEE, ARTHUR, *The King's England Series – in 41 volumes*, Hodder & Stoughton.

MESSENT, CLAUDE J. W., *A Thousand Years of Norfolk Carstone*. Published by the Author at Stibbard Rectory, Fakenham, Norfolk. (1967).

PAKINGTON, HUMPHREY, *English Villages and Hamlets*. Batsford.

PLAISTED, ARTHUR H. *English Architecture in a Country Village*. Longmans.

VALE, EDMUND, *See for Yourself*. Dent.

VALLANCE, AYMER, *Old Crosses and Lychgates*. Batsford.

VINCE, JOHN, *Farms and Farming*. Ian Allan, *Discovering Windmills*. Shire Publications. *Discovering Watermills*. Shire Publications. *Discovering Carts & Wagons*. Shire Publications. *Discovering Horse Brasses*. Shire Publications. Books for children: *Villages*. Blackwell, *History All Around You*. Wheaton.

Acknowledgements

The author gratefully acknowledges the help received from Arthur Gaunt, FRGS, Tom Parker, Frank Rodgers, Clive Street and Jeffery Whitelaw who have provided illustrations for this book. Information and permission to take other photographs has been kindly given by: Rev C. S. Jones, MA; Rev P. B. Bagnall; Michael Thomas; John Lowe, FSA; Owen J. M. Lee, BSC Agric; Cmdr O. Rodger; The Science Museum; Stanton Staveley; Avoncroft Museum of Buildings, Bromsgrove, Worcs; The Open Air Museum, Singleton, Sussex.

Information concerning the opening times of the museums mentioned in the text may be obtained from:
The Director, Avoncroft Museum of Buildings, Stoke Prior, Bromsgrove, Worcs. (Tel Bromsgrove 31363); The Director, The Open Air Museum, Duffryn, Liphook, Hants (Tel Liphook 3104).